LALIQUE

LALIQUE

JESSICA HODGE

Thunder Bay
P·R·E·S·S

ACKNOWLEDGEMENTS

The publisher wishes to thank Christie's Images, who kindly supplied most of the photography for this book.

The photograph on page 2 appears courtesy of Corbis/James L Amos.
The photograph on pages 6-7 appears courtesy of Corbis/Peter Harholdt.

All Lalique works appear courtesy of (The Lalique Estate/DACS)

Page 2: *Serpent* vase. The whole
spherical vessel, first made in 1924,
is shaped in the form of a coiled
serpent, its threatening head
resting on the narrow rim.

This edition published in 1999 by
Thunder Bay Press
5880 Oberlin Drive, Suite 400
San Diego, California 92121
1-800-284-3580

http://www.advmkt.com

Produced by PRC Publishing Ltd,
Kiln House, 210 New Kings Road, London SW6 4NZ

ISBN 1 57145 204 4

1 2 3 4 5 98 99 00 01 02

Printed and bound in China

CONTENTS

RENÉ LALIQUE

THE LONG AND FERTILE CAREER OF RENÉ LALIQUE (1860–1945) straddles not only two quite distinct crafts, those of jewelry/goldsmithing and glassmaking, but also two very different artistic styles, the florid and sensuous Art Nouveau and the disciplined and rectilinear Art Deco. As a jeweler, he created extraordinary one-of-a-kind masterpieces which are among the most original works in the medium since the Renaissance goldsmiths; as a glassmaker his work was no less technically innovative, but he also harnessed the opportunities offered by mass production to meet a much larger and more diverse market. The Armenian financier Calouste Gulbenkian, who remained a staunch supporter and admirer of the artist from their first meeting in the early 1890s, wrote to Lalique's daughter on his death:

"My admiration for his unique work has never ceased to grow during the 50 years our friendship lasted and I feel, I am absolutely convinced, that he has not yet fully received his due. His place is among the great in the history of art of all times, and his very personal mastery, his exquisite imagination, will be admired by future elites."

Certainly the jewels which Lalique created for Gulbenkian were more for show than use, but much of his later work reflected a more practical and functional emphasis.

The inspiration and motivation of this shy and private man remain something of a mystery. This was partly a conscious decision on his part; almost as soon as he had established his name as a master glassmaker, around 1912, lesser craftsmen began to pirate his ideas, and Lalique made a point of intense secretiveness about his working methods. For example, we still do not know the exact formula for the pearly opalescent glass which is one of Lalique's most familiar trademarks. He chose to keep secret the composition of all the types of glass with which he worked. When an English firm, Jobling of Sunderland, developed its own "Opalique" glass in the early 1930s and approached Lalique with a view to manufacturing Lalique's products in Great Britain on a royalty basis, the suggestion was firmly rejected.

This combination of creative originality and commercial acumen is one of Lalique's defining characteristics, and the foundation of much of his success in both the fields in which he worked.

Today Lalique is better known and more highly esteemed as a glassmaker than a jeweler, despite the fact that the firm that bears his name — and is still owned and managed by his descendants — continues to be active in both areas. In fact, however, the vast majority of the vases and other glassware for which we now prize Lalique were designed when he was over 50. In the 1890s and the first decade of the 20th century, René Lalique was widely recognized as a master jeweler whose work helped to establish and define the revolutionary new movement which we now know as Art Nouveau.

Initially Art Nouveau was simply called the "New Art," an extremely disparate movement which developed more or less independently in different parts of Europe in the late 19th century, with the single common purpose of replacing the established artistic order. Throughout the 19th century, almost every aspect of Western thought had been dominated by history; political, economic and social problems and issues, as well as artistic ones, were referred to historical precedents and

8

Above: René Lalique.

Pages 6–7: A selection of Lalique's most exquisite and characteristic products.

principles. Historical novels, such as those of Sir Walter Scott in Great Britain, James Fenimore Cooper in the US and Victor Hugo in France, were the rage; most operas had historical settings, those of Verdi being the obvious example; and sculpture and art focused on historical themes.

Among the first artists to revolt against the Victorian cult of eclecticism and revivalism were those who, in 1848 in Britain, founded the Pre-Raphaelite Brotherhood. Their aim was not to return to the art of the period before Raphael, but rather to reject academic practice — the tradition of working within one of a series of defined historical styles — and to return to Nature.

They chose their name, according to one of their number, William Holman Hunt (1827–1910), "to keep in our minds our determination ever to do battle against the frivolous art of the day." Like their Art Nouveau successors, their primary aim was to produce an aesthetic mood which owed nothing to the past. In 1851, however, the Crystal Palace exhibition demonstrated that the Industrial Revolution had added a further element to that Victorian yearning for period style so deplored by the Pre-Raphaelites. The advent of the machine provided the means to mass-produce furniture and artifacts in any of a vast range of historical styles. As late as 1899, a critic writing in the journal *L'Art Decoratif* complained:

"What do we see on every side? Wallpapers which wound the eye; against them, ornate furniture which wounds the eye; at intervals, a gaudily draped bay which wounds the eye; and every spare nook and cranny is hung with plates of spinach with decorative borders which wound the eye. Let the eye come to terms with all this as best it can."

Most of those artists and craftsmen who rejected historicism and the Victorian clutter which was its domestic expression were practitoners rather than theoreticians. It was the English teacher, writer and designer William Morris (1834–96) who, more than anyone, laid the theoretical ground for the development of Art Nouveau, with his explicit rejection of mid-Victorian aesthetic values, his espousal of the naturalism first advocated by the Pre-Raphaelities, and above all his support for and elevation of the decorative arts, then as now regarded as a poor cousin to the fine arts. This espousal of naturalism, however floridly interpreted, and the emphasis on decorative arts, are two of the few unifying elements in a movement that by the turn of the century encompassed the extraordinarily diverse work of the Scottish architect Charles Rennie Mackintosh (1868–1928), the French designer Émile Gallé (1846–1904) and the Czech painter Alphonse Mucha (1860–1939).

Another extremely influential element in the development of the new style, and one that is clearly identifiable in the work of the young Lalique, was the growing availability and appreciation of Japanese art from the mid-19th century onward. A treaty signed in 1854 between Japan and the United States swiftly led to trade agreements between Japan and the principal Western powers, and in turn to a flood of Japanese artifacts into Western markets. In terms of fine art, it was Japanese woodblock prints which had the greatest impact, with their popular — even vulgar — subject-matter, unorthodox, non-perspectival viewpoint, brilliant color and sheer vivacity. Along with prints, however, came fans, ceramics, enamelware, masks and "netsuke," or decorative toggles.

Suzanne, made in Lalique's trademark frosted and opalescent glass. The sinuous nude set against her classically-inspired drapery, here converted to a light source; is one of his most famous and prized statuettes.

One of the most enthusiastic proponents of all things Japanese was Siegfried Bing (1838–1905), a naturalized Frenchman from Hamburg, who visited Japan in 1875, and on his return opened a shop in Paris which specialized in Japanese goods. On a visit to the Columbian Exposition in Chicago in 1893, Bing met Louis Comfort Tiffany (1848–1933), the leading exponent of American Art Nouveau and son of the influential New York jeweler Charles L. Tiffany. This meeting led to a business partnership which gave Bing the opportunity of representing America's foremost decorative artist in Paris. In 1895, Bing opened his Maison Art Nouveau, with an exhibition of stained-glass windows designed by some of the foremost avant-garde artists of the day, including Toulouse-Lautrec, Vuillard and Bonnard, and executed by Tiffany in New York. Although the French continued to call the new movement "Le Style Moderne," foreign critics swifly adopted the term "Art Nouveau" to describe the furnishings and artifacts that Bing offered for sale in his new establishment.

MASTER JEWELER

Among many other artists with whom Bing was associated in the 1880s and 1890s was the young René Lalique, then a freelance jewelry designer, who opened his first workshop in 1885. Born in 1860 in the village of Ay in the département of Marne in northeastern France, some 100 miles east of Paris, René Lalique was the only child of a merchant whose business was decorative trifles, what today would be termed "novelty goods." The family moved to the outskirts of Paris when Lalique was two, but he retained his connections with the Marne region, where his mother's family remained, and returned there for holidays.

Little is known of Lalique's early years, other than that he attended school at the Lycée Turgot, near Vincennes, a northeastern suburb of Paris, where he won an award for drawing in about 1871. He clearly showed artistic promise, and was already in his early teens selling paintings of flowers and insects on ivory plaques. In 1876, when he was 16, his father died, and the young Lalique enrolled as apprentice with the successful Parisian jeweler and goldsmith Louis Aucoc (1850–1932).

Aucoc was a de luxe jeweler in the traditional style, working principally with the diamonds and other gemstones that were flooding into Europe at this time from the recently opened African mines. French jewelry toward the end of the 19th century was afflicted with the same absorption in historical revivalism that is traceable in other art forms. Imitations of Etruscan, Carolingian, Renaissance and Louis XIII originals all enjoyed brief bursts of popularity, while critics lamented the attendant lack of artistic innovation or originality. The first sign of change, heralding the development of Art Nouveau proper, came in the 1870s with the work of the renowned Second Empire jeweler Oscar Massin, who introduced an element of fluidity and naturalism into his designs. The vast majority of Parisian jewelers, however, continued to work with a limited range of largely neo-rococo motifs; the market required heavy, showy pieces, in which the gems dominated their setting, and that was what Aucoc produced. In the two years that he worked with Aucoc, Lalique would have acquired the basic jeweler's skills, and invaluable knowledge of the properties of the gems with which he worked. At the same time, however, he enrolled in the excellent École des Arts Decoratifs in Paris, suggesting that he aspired to be more than a simple technician.

In furtherance of his studies, Lalique moved in 1878 to Sydenham on the southern outskirts of London, where a large number of French emigrants had already settled. According to the memoirs of his contemporary, the goldsmith Henri Véver, he attended the "Collège de Sydenham," probably the School of Art then established in Joseph Paxton's iron-and-glass Crystal Palace, which had been constructed for the 1851 Great Exhibition and subsequently moved to Sydenham.

Sultane square box, molded with a sylized leaf motif, and with the handle formed by a seated female nude (see page 128).

Art education was at that time considerably more progressive in Great Britain than in France, largely due to the efforts of men like William Morris, and Lalique would undoubtedly have come into contact with the reverberations of the Arts and Crafts Movement of which Morris was one of the prime movers. One or two of Lalique's later creations, notably the glass and silver chalice he made in about 1904, reflect a distinctively Arts and Crafts influence.

Although — like Art Nouveau subsequently — the styles adopted by the Arts and Crafts movement were diverse, and it did not have a significant impact in France, its proponents were united in promoting the moral superiority of "honest" design and natural materials in an industrial age. Another facet of the Arts and Crafts movement that may well have attracted the young Lalique was its emphasis on fidelity to nature. At Sydenham he seems to have devoted much of his time to drawing from life and making nature studies, and proved to be a superb draftsman, as the many surviving sketches and finished drawings for his jewelry designs demonstrate.

Lalique returned to Paris in 1880, aged 20, and began a detailed study of jewelry manufacturing techniques. He also studied sculpture for a time at the École Bernard Palissey under Justin Lequien. Popular taste of the time favored the sculptors of the previous generation, such as Albert Carrier-Belleuse (1824–87) and Jean-Baptiste Carpeaux (1827–75), who worked in a decorative revivalist style which owes something to the Italian neoclassical sculptor Canova (1757–1822). The graceful poses and smooth outlines of Lalique's later figural work in glass, both his small-scale perfume bottle stoppers and the larger glass sculptures such as

Suzanne, owe something to this stage of his studies. The Palissy school also produced a line of pottery dishes and molds, decorated in relief with realistically modeled plants, fishes and reptiles, and this influence too may be traced in Lalique's use of naturalistic models bordering on the bizarre, both in his jewelry and in his glasswork.

After a brief period spent designing wallpaper and textiles, Lalique embarked, in 1881, on a career as a freelance jeweler. His early work, inevitably, was based on the traditional styles and materials that appealed to the wealthy clientele of such established jewelry houses as Aucoc, Boucheron and Cartier, all of which bought his jewelry. Although few of these early pieces survive today, they were made available to Henri Véver when he was writing the last volume of his magisterial work *La bijouterie francaise au XIXe siecle* (1908), and a number of them, dating from the period 1884–90, were reproduced in the book. These are conventional diamond-set pieces, displaying great technical facility, but none of the originality of subject-matter and innovatory technique which was to blossom in the next ten years.

In 1884, Lalique had the first opportunity to exhibit his work, a selection of watercolor jewelry designs, at an Art and Industry exhibition of contemporary goldwork, and attracted favorable comment from many visitors, including the renowned jeweler Alphonse Fouquet. In late 1885 he was able to buy his own workshop, which enabled him to manufacture as well as design jewelry, and he seems quickly to have established a successful business as a subcontractor to established firms. In 1887, he acquired a second workshop, and in 1890 he combined both workforces, around 30 people in total, in new and larger premises.

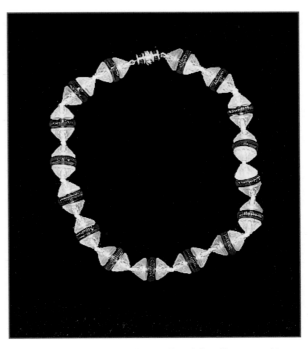

Dahlias et Rondelles Plates necklace, in frosted and blue glass, and composed of pairs of floral beads in the form of dahlias, interspersed with flat disc-shaped beads.

A turning point came in the early 1890s, when Lalique was introduced to the acclaimed actress Sarah Bernhardt (1845–1923), probably by the painter Georges Clairin, who with Alphonse Mucha designed many wardrobes and sets for Bernhardt's frequent and profitable foreign tours. Then in her late forties, Bernhardt was moving away from the "*jeune princesse*" roles of her youth and cultivating a new, more sophisticated and exotic image. She insisted on the finest quality for her costumes, and this included her stage jewelry. According to Véver,

Lalique's first work for her was a lotus corsage ornament for *Izeyl*, a play set in India, and he went on to create the jewelry for four more of her plays, as well as designing many of the jewels she wore off-stage. Sadly, little of this work survives, but the famed photographer Nadar portrayed Bernhardt in *Izeyl*, wearing Lalique's lotus corsage, and the jewel itself is in the possession of the Garrick Club, London. A huge and simple design, it is enameled a subtle gray-green with an opalescent shimmer, and is totally different in style from the traditional work Lalique had produced hitherto.

More revolutionary still were his two designs for diadems for *Theodora*, one of Bernhardt's most famous roles, in which she played the prostitute who rose to become empress, wife of the sixth-century Byzantine emperor Justinian. The designs were exhibited at the 1895 Salon of the Société des Artistes Français, the second year that Lalique had exhibited there under his own name. These included a superb tiara consisting of writhing and interlocked snakes, one of which lunged forward from the front of the tiara, while two at the side spat out great chains of pearls. Although never made as a tiara, this design was adapted by Lalique into a corsage, and was one of the most dramatic and extraordinary of all the jewels that he showed at the 1900 Paris Exposition which made his name as a jeweler.

It seems that the special requirements of stage jewelry released in Lalique the uninhibitedly dramatic approach to jewelry that was to distinguish all his subsequent work as a goldsmith. Freed from the requirement to incorporate conventional precious stones into traditional designs, he was able to explore a far wider range of materials and designs. Through Bernhardt, he met the Armenian financier Calouste Gulbenkian, millionaire, arts patron and

one of the actress's many admirers, and in about 1895 Gulbenkian commissioned the first of a series of magnificent items of jewelry, many of which are now housed in the Calouste Gulbenkian Museum, Lisbon.

One of the earliest of the Gulbenkian pieces is a hair comb designed in the form of a thistle (c.1895), made of horn, enamel and diamonds. The use of diamonds suggests that Lalique had still not wholly broken free of the need to appeal to conventional taste, but otherwise the piece is as revolutionary as the *Theodora* snake diadem, and encapsulates the originality, technical virtuosity and sheer beauty which rapidly established Lalique not only as the foremost jeweler of the day, but also as the true initiator of Art Nouveau jewelry design. The naturalism of the drooping thistle heads and the use of such novel materials as horn and enamel became essential characteristics of a new style of *bijouterie*, which regarded artistic interpretation as the true measure of a piece's worth, as against the old-fashioned *joaillier*, who was governed by the intrinsic value of his materials.

These characteristics also link Lalique's developing style with the interest in "Japonisme" already discussed. Japanese artists and craftsmen, from the master print-maker Hokusai with his "Thirty-six Views of Mount Fuji" to the humble netsuke-maker, demonstrated a passionate appreciation of the beauty of nature. Many of the more unusual naturalistic motifs, such as beetles, wasps, frogs and golden carp, that Lalique explored both in his jewelry and, later, in his glasswork, are paralleled in Japanese art. Equally his use of horn, a humble material hitherto reserved for practical and durable vessels and drinking cups, may have been inspired by Japanese craftsmen, who were skilled in the

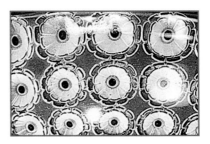

working of organic materials such as horn, ivory and tortoiseshell.

The relationship with Gulbenkian led to the creation of many of Lalique's most sumptuous and extraordinary creations. As a patron, Gulbenkian was interested in exploring the full range of his protégé's creative imagination, and he gave him a totally free hand. Released from the usual constraints of cost and wearability, Lalique created a series of one-of-a-kind pieces so daring in design and, in some cases, made in such high relief, that they would have been wholly impractical to wear. Among these are the *Serpents* corsage already referred to (c.1898), probably the most stunning of all Lalique's serpent jewels. Made in silver-gilt and *champlevé* enamel, it consists of nine interlaced snakes, each of which originally spat out a row of pearls from its threatening jaws, in a clear echo of the *Theodora* diadem. Many of Lalique's jewelry pieces, and especially those featuring sculpted insects, contain an element of the macabre. The *Beetles* brooch he made for Gulbenkian in about 1904 consists of two dark brown patinated beetles apparently locked in combat for the tourmaline that forms the centerpiece of the brooch, while a *Frog* choker (c.1900) features a young woman's smiling profile surrounded by crawling and leaping frogs.

Other well-known pieces that Lalique made for Gulbenkian include the *Peacock* and *Dragonfly* corsage ornaments (both c.1898), both reflecting the fascination with themes from the natural world which remained such a feature of his work, and both using the long-neglected art of enameling. Enamel is a form of soft glass which is fused onto a metallic surface to create a colorful and decorative effect. It offers an economical alternative to real gemstones, but it can also be used to create strikingly realistic effects. *Cloisonné* and *champlevé* enamel, both familiar in Roman and medieval as well as Renaissance Europe, were used regularly by Lalique. *Cloisonné* work involves pouring the enamel into grooves engraved on the surface of the object to be decorated, while *champlevé* features a network of metal bands which divides the enamel decoration into *cloisons* or compartments. As well as these, however, Lalique also mastered *plique à jour* enameling, familiar to Japanese craftsmen but rarer in Europe, which is similar to *cloisonné* but without the metal backing. The effect of this is to allow light to shine through the translucent enamel, creating a stained-glass effect, and Lalique recognized that this was ideal for representing the more delicate effects of the natural world, such as the veined wings of flying insects or the irridescent tracery of foliage.

The *Dragonfly* corsage is a masterpiece of *plique à jour* enameling, but it also represents an equally innovatory and rather more bizarre aspect of Lalique's work. One of the themes that appealed to the "New Art" was the female nude, with its opportunity for sinuous line and languorous mood, and Lalique may have been the first artist since the 16th-century goldsmiths to represent the nude in jewelry. Indeed the first official recognition of his outstanding talent was the third-class prize awarded him at the 1895 Société des Artistes Français exhibition for a figurative, diamond-set brooch in the Renaissance style. This figurative motif recurred constantly in his work, in later vase designs and glass sculpture as well as in jewelry. Perhaps the most outstanding early example is a remarkable pendant dating from 1900, which consists of five entwined bodies above a large baroque pearl.

Below is a selection of some of Lalique's most characteristic work from the 1920s and 1930s. From left:

Quatre Perruches clock, designed in 1920 and showing paired parakeets under a Japanese-inspired flowering cherry branch.

Blue-stained *Naïade* statuette, also from 1920, showing a kneeling mermaid holding a shell to her ear.

Nemours bowl, molded with a pattern of anemones, each with a black-enameled center.

Deux Sirènes, an unusually large (25cm diameter) box decorated with two cavorting sea-sprites, their stylized hair metamorphosing into ripples of water.

Lévrier car mascot, a flattened hemisphere molded in intaglio with the figure of a racing greyhound.

In some pieces, however, Lalique took his exploitation of the nude a stage further, by combining it with other animal forms. The *Dragonfly* corsage consists of an articulated dragonfly body, made of gold and decorated with chrysophase and dark blue enamel, from the jaws of which unnervingly emerges the head and torso of a woman, with *plique à jour* enameled wings in place of arms. The macabre effect of this design is enhanced by the vast, predatory claws which extend from the dragonfly body. An equally dramatic, but rather less disturbing, example of this theme of female metamorphosing into winged creature, is the *Swan* necklace (c.1900), comprising nine gold nudes set in green *plique à jour* enamel, with paired black-and-gold swans at their feet.

In these extraordinary pieces it is possible to trace Lalique's early sculptural studies, and some critics have suggested that, had he wished, Lalique could have been a successful sculptor. Certainly, as a jeweler, his work is remarkably free of the fussy decorative detail — for example, forms bordered with diamonds — that usually characterized the work of a master jeweler. His use of materials hitherto unknown to the jeweler, such as horn, enamel, and, increasingly, glass, offered a much greater flexibility of modeling and texture than was usual, and his jewelry designs reflected and exploited this opportunity. Other materials chosen for their aesthetic qualities rather than their intrinsic value included opals, normally avoided as unlucky, citrines, and baroque (irregularly-contoured) pearls, but Lalique also worked with the entire spectrum of gems, from diamonds and amethysts to rock crystals and the humble moonstone. Sometimes the asymmetrical design of an object was dictated by the use of semi-precious stones cut in the medieval *cabochon* style, a smooth oval, in preference to the contemporary taste for faceting.

It is this readiness to explore non-traditional materials which is perhaps the key to Lalique the designer, and which first motivated his experiments with glass, a natural development from his use of vitreous enamel. A very early product of this work is a perfume bottle and stopper (c.1893) made in glass by the *cire-perdue* or lost wax technique. The perfume bottle remained among Lalique's personal possessions until his death, and the *cire-perdue* technique was further exploited in the early 1900s, as he turned his attention increasingly away from jewelry and toward glasswork. Most of Lalique's work with glass in the 1890s, however, involved powdered glass, often colored, which was fired in a mold and then lightly enameled, a process known as *pâte-de-verre*.

Cast *pâte-de-verre* shapes were used to create a hybrid form of jewelry which, though popular at the time, is perhaps less satisfactory to the modern eye. The *Winter Woodland* pendant (1899–1900) consists of a misty miniature landscape of frost-covered trees and lake, cast in ice-blue glass, set in an enameled frame in the shape of a snow-laden tree, from the bare roots of which dangle a single baroque pearl. The result is curious rather than aesthetically pleasing, an admittedly rare example of the technician's enthusiasm overcoming the designer's better judgment. The piece is interesting for another reason, however, in that it is one of the few pieces bought by Gulbenkain which also exists in other versions.

A later and more successful example of the use of glass in jewelry is the *Rose Branches* corsage ornament (c.1905–10), also in the Gulbenkian collection, which features a large amethyst at its center, set on a realistically thorny rose branch made in gold and enamel, and which in turn supports two heavily drooping clusters of molded pink glass roses. In 1904, Lalique acquired a new patron, the American Henry Walters, who bought a number of pieces from the exhibit of Lalique's work at the Saint Louis World's Fair, including the magnificently realistic *Grape* and *Vine* necklaces, both incorporating elements of subtly-colored frosted and cast glass.

Undoubtedly the high moment of Lalique's

From left to right: *Le Jade*, in the shape of a Chinese snuff bottle; *Amphitrite*, the bottle shaped as a shell, the stopper a kneeling female nude; *Feuilles stylisées*, with a flower and leaf design.

14

career as a master jeweler came at the Exposition Internationale Universelle, held in Paris in 1900. This commemorated the 30th aniversary of the Third Republic with displays of recent technological advances and contemporary art and design. For his exhibit, Lalique designed a *vitrine* or display cabinet which was itself an Art Nouveau masterpiece, with patinated bronze grillwork and five sinuous female nudes set against a backdrop of feathery wings which trailed far below their feet. In this spectacular setting Lalique's sumptuous jewels, including a number of horn combs ornamented with precious stones, and a *Cock's Head* diadem, as well as the *Dragonfly* and *Serpent* corsages already described, were hailed by contemporary critics as among the most arresting attractions at the fair. The critic Gabriel Mourey wrote that Lalique had "entirely renovated the art of the goldsmith," and the result was to disseminate his fame not just through Europe but also to the U.S. Further displays of his work followed in Turin (1902), the St. Louis World's Fair (1904), the Liège fair (1905), and in London (1903 and 1905).

The 1905 London exhibition, held at the prestigious Agnew gallery, was the first to include a representative sample of Lalique's goldsmithing work other than jewelry, such as a number of decorative boxes, directly descended from 18th-century work, but displaying all the technical and decorative brilliance of his jewelry. Other *objets de vertu* which fell within his range as a goldsmith and were exhibited at Agnews were decorative daggers made of horn; statuettes; purses; salt and pepper mills; and silver table pieces. The focal point of the exhibition was a large silver centerpiece, over 24 inches high, the central motif of which was a naked water nymph draped in seaweed and standing on a

water lily. She stood on a silver base set in glass, in imitation of a pond, and round the rim were four other nymphs, holding fishes from whose mouths poured a cascade of molded glass. London critics were not wholly favorable in their reception, one condemning the "unpleasant decadence" suggested by some of Lalique's juxtapositions of natural forms in "unnatural-looking material," but by this time his position as the Art Nouveau jeweler *par excellence* was too well established to be challenged.

MASTER GLASSMAKER

The craft of glassmaking showed the influence of the "New Art" considerably earlier than that of jewelry, probably because there was no equivalent deep-rooted traditional style to overcome. In the late 1870s, Eugene Rousseau was already experimenting with cloudy, aerated and crackled internal effects, metal oxides suspended within the glass, and naturalistic relief images chiseled deep into the surface. From about 1884, however, it was the formidably creative designer and entrepreneur Émile Gallé who led the field in French glassmaking. Inheriting a decorative glassware business from his father in 1874, Gallé built the firm into one of the largest in Europe, while at the same time pursuing his own experimental work, which resulted in a comparatively small number of prestige creations unrivaled both for their invention and for their technical brilliance.

The inspiration behind Gallé's work was the realization that, rather than a clear, colorless and static substance, glass was an infinitely variable medium which could be engraved, colored, enameled and ornamented to achieve an extraordinary range of complex internal patterns, simulated movement, and surface textures. By the time of his

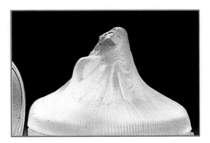

Lalique's partnership with Coty led him to design a large number of perfume bottles, for Coty and other perfumiers. Below, left to right:

Althea, the bottle is a stylized flowerhead, the stopper is two bees.

Fleurs concaves, from 1912, a tapering cylindrical bottle with stylized flowerheads inset into the glass.

Roses, is a globular bottle with a feather design, and a stopper in the form of a classical nymph.

Ambre d'Orsay, in dark amethyst glass, the corners feature nymphs.

Le Jade, a pale green bottle in the shape of a Chinese snuff bottle.

Amphitrite, is gray-stained glass in the shape of a shell, the stopper is a kneeling female nude.

Feuilles stylisées, is molded with a pattern of leaves, while the stopper has bands of stylized flowerheads.

Tête Femme powder box made for Coty in 1912, with both the box and lid molded with vertical ridges, from which emerges the barely-delineated head and shoulders of a woman.

A variety of Lalique's floral and foliate designs. Clockwise from far left:

Chypre, a cylindrical bottle decorated with rows of flowerheads.

Soucis, in amber glass, a seal in the form of a vase of flowers.

Cactus atomizer, in frosted and black-enameled glass.

Je Reviens perfume bottle.

Dahlia, two bottles, each modeled as a single flowerhead.

Replique, molded as an acorn with a silvered metal stopper.

Another example of *Chypre* and a spherical version with sunflowers.

Deux Fleurs, formed by two flowerheads and a seedhead stopper.

death in 1904, Gallé's factory employed some 300 people, had retail outlets in Paris, London and Frankfurt, and had established a successful line in series-produced vases and table-lamps. His artistic achievement, however, is measured rather by the one-of-a-kind pieces that he created for major exhibitions or public commissions. By contrast, Lalique succeeded in adapting his creative genius to the requirements of mass manufacture, while at the same time retaining the high design standards that he had set himself in his goldsmithing work.

Gallé's primary inspiration was nature, and his glassware paralleled Lalique's jewelry of much the same date in its exploitation of floral and animal themes; like Lalique, his use of creatures such as dragonflies, beetles and ants sometimes bordered on the macabre. His success inspired a host of imitators, some, such as the Daum *frères*, proving almost as innovatory as Gallé himself, while in the U.S. the market was almost wholly dominated by Louis Comfort Tiffany. Toward the end of the century, the traditional art of *pâte-de-verre*, glass which had been ground and refired in a mold, was re-established by the French sculptor Henri Cros (1840–1907), who used it to make large reliefs. This was taken up for the production of glass vessels by a new generation of glassmakers in the 1890s, and also, as we have seen, by the young Lalique. Thus by the time that Lalique began to turn his attention to glass as a medium in its own right, rather than as an additional decorative element in jewelry design, a successful and innovative glass industry was already well established.

Lalique's career as a glassmaker, like his jewelry, developed in the way it did as much through a series of chances as through any clear design on the part of the artist. As well as his experiments with

pâte-de-verre and *cire-perdue* in the 1890s, he also made a small number of frosted glass relief plaques. Toward the end of the decade he was casting larger panels in glass and beginning to exhibit bas-reliefs in translucent glass. In 1902, he set up an experimental glassworks on the family estate at Clairfontaine, about 24 miles south-west of Paris, where the glass was made from raw materials. This replaced the vitreous blocks bought for the Paris workshop, which was at the turn of the century still mainly devoted to goldsmithing. At Clairfontaine, Lalique increased the scale of the molds he used for making glass plaques, and designed and made his first decorative architectural panels.

Meanwhile his Paris business had again outgrown its premises, and toward the end of 1902 Lalique moved his operations to a large and impressive building in the Cours de la Reine, near the Place de la Concorde. He supervised the renovation of this himself, incorporating not only workshops, but also exhibition and retail space and living quarters, and designing many of the details, including the staircase. This remained his Paris base for the rest of his life, but in 1905 a separate retail outlet was opened in the Place Vendôme. For the main entrance to the Cours de la Reine building, Lalique designed and made metal-framed doors, glazed with unique frosted glass panels which were decorated with pine branches cast in shallow relief. This was Lalique's first large-scale use of architectural glass, a field in which he was to receive a number of major commissions in the 1920s and 1930s. The door to the display room also incorporated glass panels, this time depicting classical male nudes, and Lalique also designed chandeliers and furniture, including a work table, desk and chairs. A photograph of the exhibition gallery dating from

about 1905 shows the magnificent Agnew's silver centerpiece in pride of place. Clearly Lalique was already intent on extending the range of his activities, but at this stage glass was only one of several media in which he was experimenting.

The expanded workshop premises allowed Lalique to increase production to meet the demands created by his success at the 1900 Exposition, and while the emphasis continued to be on jewelry, he began to introduce new objects such as statuettes and vessels in glass and metal. Most of these were unique items which continued to reflect the decorative themes of his jewelry work — for example a superb sugar bowl made of opaque green glass, blown into a silver armature featuring the familiar writhing serpent motif — but within a few years Lalique also began to manufacture some pieces in series.

One of these, a chalice made in glass and silver (c.1904), is a particularly interesting example of the interface between the jeweler and the glassmaker, the Art Nouveau and the Art Deco designer. The chalice consists of a metal armature shaped in a pine-branch design similar to that on the Cours de la Reine doors. The style of this, with its interlocking network of branches and closely observed pinecones, is closer to the Celtic-inspired repertoire of the Arts and Crafts movement than to the more florid Art Nouveau manner of much of Lalique's jewelry, and already hints at the simplification of line which was to be a necessary characteristic of his mass-produced work. The glass is free-blown, although Lalique's first mold-blown vases followed soon after, and is a milky, opalescent color which was to become one of Lalique's characteristic trademarks. Several identical examples survive, each with its control number, the highest known being 32.

Soon after opening his glass workshop at Clairfontaine, Lalique began to use the *cire perdue* or lost wax technique to produce detailed smallscale sculpted work. At this early stage in his experiments he created bronze as well as glass pieces; the armatures for objects such as the chalice and sugar bowl described above would have been made by the *cire perdue* method. Among early glass sculptures made this way are a number of exquisite figurines, generally of a single female nude, although one or two groups survive, including the lyrical *Maiden on a Dolphin* (c.1907–09) in the Gulbenkian Collection. As well as sculptures, he also experimented with a number of vase shapes using the same method, and continued to produce *cire perdue* blown vases until the late 1920s. Early one-of-a-kind *cire perdue* vases, now among the most sought-after in his oeuvre, feature many of the motifs that had inspired works of *bijouterie* in the previous decade. Examples are a *Dragonfly* vase (c.1910–13), now in the Metropolitan Museum, New York, and Gulbenkian's extraordinary *Medusa* vase (c.1909–10), on which miniature male nudes twist and cower in the snake's head tresses of the four Medusa heads which protrude from the body of the vase. The heads were cast separately in pink-tinted glass and applied to the vase when cool, a technique which Lalique first used in jewelry design and rarely applied to vase designs.

The *cire perdue* method of sculpting is by its nature laborious and time-consuming. First a design was carved by hand in modeling wax, then this maquette was encased in a semi-plastic clay mixture, which was allowed to harden, so that the finest details of the wax mold were transferred to its inner wall. The wax was then melted out (hence the term lost wax) and molten glass was poured into

the clay shell, creating a solid glass sculpture. For a vase, the glass was blown into the shell rather than poured, in order to achieve a hollow vessel. Although Lalique continued to make the occasional *cire perdue* piece throughout his career, with quite a substantial group dating from the 1920s, the future lay with different production methods.

The stimulus needed to explore a less labor-intensive method of creating glassware came from an unexpected source. In 1906 the brilliantly successful Corsican entrepreneur François Coty

(1874–1934) opened an establishment in the immediate neighborhood of Lalique's newly acquired retail premises in the Place Vendôme. Coty, arriving in Paris in 1900, had recognized and seized an opening in the marketing of perfumes and cologne. Most perfumes were still expensively blended by chemists and dispensed in plain pharmaceutical bottles, but the discovery of synthetic ingredients, which were far cheaper than the natural products used hitherto, led to the production of large quantities of good-quality perfume at

18

a reasonable price. In 1904 Coty had founded the House of Coty to market these in a more attractive manner, and his eye may have been caught by the small decorative flasks and bottles that were sometimes included in the display gallery at the adjacent Lalique premises. In 1907 he asked his neighbor to design labels for his perfume bottles, and soon after he commissioned Lalique to create the bottles themselves.

The first perfume bottles that Lalique created for Coty were produced at the glassworks of Legras and Company. Perhaps the earliest, dating from around 1908, is also one of the most dramatic in design, featuring a sinuous female nude who twines out of a lily flower. Below her the words "*L'Effleurt de Coty*" are molded. By 1910, however, Lalique's bottles for Coty were being made at the glassworks at Combs-la-Ville, 36 miles east of Paris, which Lalique first rented in 1909 and then bought outright in 1910. The area had long been attractive to glassmakers for its sand, which had a high silica content. Glass is made from silica melted at high temperature with a flux such as soda or lead oxide. When it is molten it can be drawn into long threads, blown into bubbles or molded. It can be colored by the addition of metallic oxides to the mixture before it is heated, or it can be painted or engraved once it has cooled.

Lalique's early designs for Coty were extraordinarily varied. *Cyclamen* (1909) is an elongated hexagonal form, tapering toward the neck and with a flat circular stopper. It is decorated on each facet with a hovering female nude, who holds up a flower, and whose long, delicately-membraned wings trail to the foot of the bottle. Similarly Art Nouveau in design, and reflecting Lalique's continuing fascination with insect life, is *Cigales*

(c.1911–12), rectangular in shape and with cicadas clinging, wings closed, to each of the four corners. By contrast, *Ambre Antique* (c.1910), a simple cylinder, is decorated with a procession of soberly-draped neoclassical female figures, while *Au Coeur des Calices* (1912) is unusual in shape, being flat and domed, and is made from a delicate blue glass which is darkest at the top, where the stopper is a single plump bumblebee.

The success of the Lalique/Coty partnership, and the varied range of designs that Lalique was inspired to produce, necessitated a sophisticated and efficient process of manufacture if the market was to be met. It has been estimated that Lalique initially employed between 50 and 100 people at Combs-la-Ville, and he at once introduced the latest technological advances in glassmaking, including the use of precision-cast metal molds, in place of clay or wood, to ensure a high-quality product, and semi-automated molding processes.

He also favored a lead oxide content of only about 12 percent, roughly half of what was required under French law for his glass to be termed "lead crystal." The resulting *demi-cristal* was less clear and sparkling, less crisply-molded and sharp-edged, than the true crystal, and has sometimes been criticized as rough and undistinguished; one critic declared that Lalique's fame rested "more on his ability as a mold-maker than that of a glass-maker, for his metal left much to be desired." From Lalique's point of view, however, demi-crystal had great advantages: it was relatively inexpensive and therefore well suited to mass production; it was highly malleable in its semi-molten state and unlikely to adhere to the mold during cooling; and it required little surface treatment on removal from the mold.

Lalique designed at least 16 perfume bottles for Coty, and continued to create related objects such as stoppers, boxes, testers and labels for him until well into the 1930s. Soon, however, he also began to market perfume bottles under his own name, and in 1913 was commissioned by the established perfumer D'Orsay to design some of their bottles. As the new century progressed, a new artistic style had begun to emerge in the decorative arts, partly in reaction to the voluptuous excesses of Art Nouveau. This was retrospectively christened Art Deco by art historians, after the 1925 Paris *Exposition des Arts Décoratifs et Industrielles* which came to be seen as its moment of glory, and the chronological dividing line between the two styles is usually taken as World War I. In fact, however, Art Deco had its roots in the period 1908–12, and was in many ways an extension rather than an abandonment of Art Nouveau, sharing its preoccupation with lavish ornamentation, fine materials and exquisite craftsmanship, but with a greater emphasis on stylization, simplification and geometric rather than vegetal motifs. What distinguished it above all from its predecessor was the belief that form should follow function, and its espousal of mass production.

Émile Gallé, the great exponent of Art Nouveau glass in France, had died in 1904 and, while Maurice Marinot (1882–1960), a Fauve painter turned glass artist, succeeded him as the premier studio glassmaker of the next three decades, Lalique demonstrated that it was possible to manufacture art glass without compromising its quality. Unlike Gallé, he showed no particular interest in experimenting with the chemistry of glass, and his basic range of materials was fairly limited, the two most characteristic being the milky opalescent glass

for which he is perhaps most prized today, and a clear colorless glass, either frosted or polished. Guillaume Janneau, in his seminal book *Modern Glass* (1931), described the two masters in the following terms:

"His (Gallé's) complicated and skilled productions, in which the substance itself was disguised, were regarded, not without reason, as masterpieces in the technical sense. In this direction every possibility had been exhausted. No one could carry the art further than Gallé, whose magic touch transformed glass into precious stones. Lalique, however, revealed the beauty of glass as glass. His relief technique, with its adroitly selected design, gave full effect to rich material and rare craftsmanship. In a style which was altogether French . . . he created a formula no less exquisite than that of Murano."

In 1911 the Société des Artistes Decorateurs opened its new salon with an exhibition of glass in what was described at the time as "the modern style," and in the following year Lalique exhibited some of his mold-blown products at the same venue. These met with immediate approval; the critic Nilsen Lauvrik wrote that his "accomplished craftsmanship has enabled him to utilize the services of the machine without in the least affecting the artistic quality of his products . . . it has become a tool of the artist whereby he may communicate his ideas to a greater number than was ever possible to the craftsman of old." From descriptions of the work shown, it seems that this included a range of simple, inexpensive items for the home, such as carafes and decanters, drinking vessels, and articles such as inkwells, paperweights and seals, as well as perfume bottles.

The selection below shows the range of Lalique's themes, from classically-influenced designs to stylized birds. Clockwise from left:

Pan perfume bottle, in clear, frosted and sepia-stained glass, molded on the shoulders with four pan masks and floral garlands. The stopper is a bouquet of flowers.

Hirondelles bottle with swallows also featured on a vase, car mascot, picture frame and clock.

Lacdor bottle, made for Lubin in 1920.

Panier des Roses bottle, modeled in the shape of a tall openwork basket from which roses spill out at the top, forming the rim and the stopper.

Statuette drapée seal, in the form of a semi-draped woman.

19

Lalique is now best-known for his vases although he did not start producing them until late in his career. The examples above show (from left):

Chevreuse, a frosted and sepia-stained vase molded with protruding bands of small flowers.

Vichy, a clear glass vase each side molded in low relief with swags of roses and foliage.

Orly, a clear vase with four arched handles each molded with radiating ovals.

20

It is somewhat ironic that Lalique is best known today for his vases, since he did not design one for commercial production until he was over 50, and the great majority of them were made in his sixties and seventies. The first vases that he made were mold-blown, like the perfume bottles for Coty and other perfume houses, and the earliest recorded examples date from 1912, when Lalique held an exhibition of his new art forms in glass at his Place Vendôme showrooms. These are transitional pieces, in the sense that they combine mechanical production with a degree of hand-finishing. One of them, molded with low-relief lily pads, has the same swelling form as the *Medusa* vase, and features green glass frogs applied at the shoulder after the molding process was completed.

Among the first production mold-blown pieces were the *Courges* (Gourds) and *Monnaie du Pape* (Honesty leaves) vases, both made around 1913. These have the characteristic mold-blown shape of narrow neck and swelling body. The latter also features the heavy *patiné* characteristic of this early period of manufacture, a means of adding color by covering the vase with an enamel solution, which was wiped away from the relief surface as it began to dry, and then fixed with an additional low-temperature firing. *Patiné* was thus a method of external decoration, and although Lalique

continued to use it occasionally for the next 20 years, it was in a sense a throwback to the enamelwork with which he had embellished his jewelry.

By contrast, the *Courges* vase was made in a wide range of colors, including red, green, yellow, plum and turquoise, but these were achieved by adding metal oxides to the basic mix before firing: cobalt for blue, uranium for yellow, chromium for red. In the 1920s an extensive range of colored pieces was produced, and today these are particularly prized by collectors.

The surprising fact is, however, that over 90 percent of Lalique's production-ware in the 1920s and 1930s was made in his trademark pearly opalescent glass. Opalescent glass had first been made in Venice in the early 16th century and had subsequently spread through Europe, becoming a common feature of French 19th-century glass.

It is made by adding phosphates to the glass mixture, sometimes with a little cobalt to achieve a bluish sheen, and the density of the opalescence depends on the rate at which the surface cools in relation to the center. Thus the thicker the glass the richer and pearlier the effect, a characteristic which Lalique exploited in both his vases and statuettes; the opalescence is more intense on those parts of an object which are molded in relief.

MASS PRODUCTION

World War I imposed a hiatus on Lalique's creative output. Glass production ceased at Combs-la-Ville in 1915, and the factory only opened again in 1919. In that same year, Lalique exhibited in several European countries, including a large display at the Museum of Industrial Arts in Copenhagen, and he also mounted his first foray to the United States, with simultaneous exhibitions at the Knoedler Galleries and the Brooklyn Museum in New York. The result was a huge expansion in business; France might be battered and Germany crushed, but a newly affluent society was emerging in parts of Europe and in America, with a healthy appetite for the elegant and decorative.

Initially Lalique continued to limit his output to the one-of-a-kind *cire perdue* work, the perfume bottles, desk and dressing table accessories, table glass and vase designs, which had constituted the bulk of his pre-war products. The growing international market, however, prompted a corresponding expansion in his operations, and almost at once he began to plan a new glassworks. This was located in the Alsace region of France, formerly a German province and an area which benefited from government incentives to industry after the war. The factory, in the small town of Wingen-sur-Moder, has continued to operate up to the present. While Combs-la-Ville continued to concentrate on short-run or unique pieces, the new Alsatian factory was consciously planned to produce high-quality designs at modest prices. Between 1920 and 1930, Lalique tripled his work force and increased his glass production tenfold.

The major technical innovation at Wingen, and a crucial factor in the expansion of Lalique's market, was the development of the technique of press-molding, first used in 1921. This revolutionary and economical method enabled glass vessels to be produced without the need for glass-blowing. Instead the molten glass was poured directly into metal molds, where it was forced into the required shape by means of a vertical plunger. Press-molded vases are therefore recognizable by their downward tapering shape; the neck has to be the widest part to allow the entry and removal of the plunger. Until now most of Lalique's vase designs had adopted the narrow-necked bulbous shape which is readily produced by the mold-blown process and which is also typical of Japanese vase forms.

The adoption of a new production process thus dictated a change of style, and some of Lalique's finest designs from the 1920s resulted from the use of the press, despite the inevitable stylistic limitations that this imposed. As well as their different shape, however, press-molded vases are also more crisply sculpted, owing to the force with which the plunger thrusts the molten glass into the mold, and they have an even inner surface, whereas in mold-blown work the inner surface tends to follow the contours of the exterior relief decoration.

Between 1920 and 1930 Lalique designed over 200 vases, as well as introducing many other forms of glassware, almost all of which were put into production at Wingen. Press-molding proved particularly suited to the sharp geometrical motifs characteristic of Art Deco art, and vases such as *Tourbillons* (Whirlwind) and *Moissac*, both first made c.1925, demonstrate how Lalique adapted his technical and artistic skills both to his new production method and to the taste of the day. *Tourbillons* in particular has been hailed as an Art Deco masterpiece. From about 1920, designs showed an increasing tendency toward repeating or symmetrical patterns, but it is difficult to chart this development with certainty, because vase and other designs were often manufactured unchanged over an extensive period. Among the earliest products of the new factory were a number of mold-blown pieces, many of them decorated with organic or naturalistic patterns evocative of Lalique's earlier work. One of the earliest of these was the *Sauterelles* (Grasshoppers) vase, probably first made c.1921 and which continued to be reproduced until at least 1930, in clear, opalescent and colored glass.

The vase designs that Lalique produced during this incredibly fertile decade, when he was already over 60, reflected in modified form many of the themes and motifs which had fascinated him in his earliest days as a jeweler. Perhaps the richest source of creativity in his vase work were the floral and vegetal themes which he had experimented with as a student. A simple feather-like leaf might decorate a cylindrical vase (*Eucalyptus*, c.1922) or billow and overlap on a globular form (*Palmes*, c.1926), or the leaf might be almost unrecognizable, as on *Moissac*, where it lies in carefully ordered semi-abstract triangles. *Oran* (c.1925) features plump, stylized, neatly furled chrysanthemums, while *Prunes* (c.1924) is molded with thick leaf-and-fruit clusters and *Oranges* (c.1925) with striated semi-abstract leaves and ornamentally-arranged fruit. Another familiar theme is that of animal life. The golden carp which was such a feature of Japanese art continued to appear, notably in the *Formosa* vase of c.1929, available in green, orange, yellow and red glass as well as the standard opalescent. Birds might take the form of the *Tourterelles* vase and cover (c.1920), with its pair of loving and naturalistic turtle doves, or the much more stylized and

energetic cockerels which peck their way round the *Bresse* vase (1932). Generally speaking, the creatures which Lalique chose to depict in the 1920s and 1930s are the more graceful and exotic animals and birds associated with the so-called "age of elegance," but occasionally he reverted to the more grotesque decoration of his earlier work, as in the *Gros Scarabes* vase (c.1924) with its pattern of stylized beetles. The *Serpent* vase from the same date illustrates the evolution that had taken place in Lalique's treatment of his animal themes; in place of the savagingly biting but fundamentally

decorative serpents that featured on his jewelry and metalwork in the pre-war period, this piece is designed as a single coiled snake which constitutes both the form and the decoration of the vase, a classic Art Deco concept.

The sinuous nudes which had decorated Lalique's Art Nouveau jewelry also reappear in rather more corporeal and neoclassical form on a number of vases. *Archers* (c.1922) features muscular bowmen aiming their arrows at the huge birds which soar across the vessel's shoulder; *Danaides* (c.1920) has a row of stylized nymphs emptying their water urns; while the female nudes on *Bacchantes* (c.1924) are molded in high relief to give an almost Rodinesque physicality and eroticism. Purely geometric motifs also figure in Lalique's work in the 1920s, becoming much more frequent in the 1930s; an early and outstanding example is the *Nanking* vase (c.1928), with its faceted triangular decoration.

Both the Combs-la-Ville and the Wingen glassworks continued to turn out perfume bottles through the 1920s, most of which were sold empty under Lalique's own name, although he continued to work for some of the principal perfume houses, creating his classic bottle *L'Imprudence* for Worth in 1929. One particularly distinctive group are named for their overflowing horseshoe-shaped stoppers (*bouchons*) in French; *Bouchon Cassis* is decorated with plump blackcurrants, occasionally of red glass, while *Bouchon Fleur de Pommier* is an exquisite stylized flowering apple tree.

At Wingen the techniques for casting glass for this kind of solid sculptural work were greatly improved, and Lalique was able to work on a larger scale. Among the earliest and most successful results were the statuettes *Suzanne* and *Thaïs*, both

first made c.1922–23 and manufactured until the mid-1930s. Generally made in opalescent glass (although a few amber examples are known), these proved ideal for display under illumination, and were sometimes supplied with decorative brass illuminating stands. Illuminated plaques of this type were known as *surtouts*; one of the largest and rarest, over three feet in width, is a shallow fan shape decorated with three peacocks, while the *Firebird surtout* is among the most famous of all Lalique's large-scale work.

As well as illuminated sculpture, Lalique was among the first to respond to the rapid spread of domestic electricity after the war, by establishing a new line in lighting manufacture. The earliest table lamps made at Wingen were heavily ornamented sculptural creations in their own right, but Lalique soon recognized that functionality was the key to successful lighting manufacture, and concentrated his skills on creating lamps, chandeliers and wall brackets which orchestrated the light to both decorative and practical effect. Some of the lamps, such as *Apple Blossom* and *Japanese Hawthorn* (both c.1920), echo on a larger scale the design of the *Bouchon* series of perfume bottles, and consist of an illuminated base and overflowing tiara-style "stopper." This form of "caged" lighting, with the naked lightbulb concealed within a diffusing medium, became increasingly popular, and Lalique applied the same principal to ceiling lights. His *plafonniers* or light bowls could be either hung from or attached directly to the ceiling, so that the light they emitted was reflected off the ceiling. More dramatic were his *lustres* or chandeliers, perhaps his greatest contribution to interior lighting, ranging from geometric globes to massive, futuristic, many-armed creations.

Closely related to his sculptural work, but on a smaller scale, was the series of car mascots which Lalique began to produce in the mid-1920s, again demonstrating his awareness of market trends. The form was not wholly novel — the famous Rolls-Royce mascot had been designed in 1911 — but mascots were usually made in chromium-plated metal and were often simply the manufacturer's logo. The *Cinq Chevaux* mascot that Lalique was commissioned to design for Citroen in 1925 was followed by a series of about 20, all designed in the next five years, including the characteristically Art Deco *Victoire*, with its streamlined form and intimations of speed, as well as the more naturalistic *Peacock Head* and *Goldfish* mascots.

The range of Lalique's activities in these years remained extraordinarily wide. He designed clocks, furniture, perfume burners, mirrors, paperweights, jewelry, ashtrays and boxes, all in his chosen medium of glass. And yet by far the largest proportion of his commercial production in the 1920s took the form of functional tableware, including bowls, platters, decanters, carafes and glasses, all made in press-molded glass and designed to meet the post-War demand for economically-priced, non-crystal pieces. He had designed and manufactured drinking glasses since about 1905, but it was only in the 1920s that the demand became great enough to warrant commercial production.

The first commission came in 1924, from the wine merchant Cusenier, for whom Lalique designed two carafes, and thereafter he created a number of *grande cérémonie* or full table services, consisting of decanter, water goblet, three sizes of wine glass and champage goblet, as well as single items. Plates and shallow bowls were cheap and easy to manufacture, requiring a single pressing and

little hand finishing. Most of Lalique's plate designs were symmetrical or radiating in pattern, such as the *Martigues* bowl with its interlocking fish, or the stylized scallop shell on the *Coquilles* plate, which was also used on a hanging light fitting. Despite the vast range and scale of his output, Lalique ensured consistency both of quality and style by continuing to function as his expanding company's sole designer, until joined by his son Marc in the 1930s.

Lalique found a valuable forum for his new designs at the many national and international exhibitions held in the 1920s. By far the most significant of these was the Exposition des Arts Décoratifs et Industriels, held in Paris in 1925, which marked both the high point of Art Deco as a movement, and the pinnacle of Lalique's success as a glassmaker. Although 21 countries participated, it was principally a showcase for French decorative art, and Lalique's work featured throughout. The magnificent entrance gate was flanked by panels of Lalique's frosted glass, while the centerpiece of the site was a huge fountain designed by Lalique, over 40 feet high, consisting of 17 tiers of frosted glass panels, each tier bearing eight *Source de la Fontaine* statuettes. This spectacular construction, which came to symbolize the exhibition, was illuminated both from within and from below, while water cascaded out and down from the topmost tier. Other fountain commissions followed: at the Rond-Point of the Champs-Elysées in Paris; in Marseille; and at the 1931 *Daily Mail* Ideal Home Exhibition in London.

Lalique's production glass was featured in many different sections of the 1925 Exposition. His perfume bottles were prominently displayed in the *parfumerie* section; many of his large vases and lighting fixtures were included in room settings

The breadth of Lalique's production range can be seen below (from left):

Inséparables clock, decorated with two pairs of realistically detailed lovebirds perched on blossoming branches.

Ambre d'Orsay perfume bottle in black glass, each corner molded

with the figure of a draped classical female figure.

Quatre Soleils, an amber-tinted bulbous bottle molded with four chrysanthemum flowerheads on a gold foil backing; a perfume bottle designed for Coty which still has its *Eau de Coty* printed label.

Longchamps car mascot.

Some of Lalique's smaller product ranges are shown below. Clockwise from bottom:

Sanglier car mascot, modeled in the form of a wild boar and the same in gray glass.

Deux Aigles paperweight, 1914, showing two stylized eagle heads holding a ball in their beaks.

Six Figurines goblet in clear, frosted and blue-stained glass, intaglio-molded with six classical female figures in a rectangular frame.

Tête de l'Aigle seal in the form of an eagle's head.

24

exhibited by interior designers; and his tableware was displayed in a small purpose-built showroom. His own pavilion was designed in a starkly modernist style, and mainly featured *cire perdue* glass and a number of unique exhibition pieces. As well as this, however, Lalique was commissioned to design a dining room for the Sèvres pavilion, creating a room whose marble walls were incised with forest trees through which raged a boar hunt, and whose ceiling was coffered in the Italian Renaissance manner, but with coffers and beams made of glass. Along with the Sèvres porcelain on the table were wine glasses and candlesticks in molded glass by Lalique. There could be no clearer indication of the esteem in which he was held.

The use of glass in an architectural context had interested Lalique at least as early as 1902, when he designed his Cours de la Reine workshop and home, and in 1912 he had made an exhibition salon entirely in glass for François Coty, which had been shipped to New York. It was the 1925 Exposition that offered him the opportunity to further explore the architectural potential of the medium, and this time on a monumental scale. The result was a number of major commissions, of which perhaps the most spectacular was the lighting and wall-paneling for the first-class dining room on the *Normandie*, the most sophisticated passenger liner of the age. The room was more than 300 foot long, and to subdivide this immense space Lalique designed two rows of six free-standing, tiered, illuminated glass pillars. The walls were covered with rough unpolished glass, the coffered ceiling was inlaid with illuminated panels, and at each end of the room hung a huge chandelier, consisting of four tiers of vertical panels molded in zigzag lines. The building of the *Normandie* was

underwritten by the French government, which hoped that she would lure wealthy Americans to France. She made her maiden voyage in 1935, but was requisitioned by the US government in 1942 as a troops carrier, and was burnt out and sunk while being stripped out for service.

In 1933, in recognition of his long and productive career, Lalique was accorded the honor of a retrospective exhibition by the Société des Arts Décoratifs, the first such in the institution's history. This included examples of his most recent vases, as well as a selection of jewelry, tableware and furniture. A highlight of the exhibition was a glass altar, the altar rail decorated with frosted-glass lilies, and the reredos with six angels. The exhibition led to greatly increased American interest in Lalique's work, although he had already undertaken a number of major commissions, including architectural glass panels for the Oviatt building in Los Angeles (1928), and the entrance lobby for John Wanamaker's department store in Philadelphia (1932). In 1935, Altman's department store in New York mounted a major display of Lalique's glass, including architectural designs as well as smallscale pieces, and four years later Saks Fifth Avenue followed suit.

In general, however, the 1930s showed an inevitable decline in Lalique's creativity. He was 70 years old in 1930, and still leading the Lalique Company as its sole designer, but his hands were arthritic, and perhaps for that reason *cire perdue* work ceased in that year. Cost factors in production were becoming increasingly important, and items or techniques that were labor-intensive or high in overheads were discontinued. This included the manufacture of large chandeliers, mold-blown vases and *surtouts*, the use of colored glass,

and the introduction of new designs. Instead the company concentrated on press-molded vases, and the trend was toward cheaper models which stayed in production for only a limited period. The purely ornamental vase was becoming less fashionable, and designs became simple and linear, but Lalique continued to create some interesting and innovatory pieces, such as the *Actinia* vase (1934).

Perhaps the most challenging and exciting commission of the decade, and a fitting one with which to round off such a formidable career, was the renovation of St. Matthew's Church at Millbrook, near St. Helier on the island of Jersey in the English Channel. This, which can still be seen today, was carried out in conjunction with the British architect A. B. Grayson, and was one of the largest architectural commissions Lalique ever undertook. The vestibule doors contain two vast vertical glass panels, each featuring a seven-foot-tall angel, hands held in prayer, head crowned with feathers, robe falling in four panels of fluted folds. In the body of the church the central feature is a 15-foot tall glass cross, sculpted in relief with Jersey lilies, and flanked by two glass pillars similarly decorated. The altar rail, made of glass panels, again bears the lily pattern, as do the screens which form the chancel and enclose the vestry on one side of the altar and the Lady Chapel on the other. In this side chapel is another altar made entirely of plain glass panels, above which stands a reredos screen constructed of tall relief panels showing four monumental angels. The glass font, the tall side windows and the light fittings are all also by Lalique.

In 1937, however, the Combs-la-Ville glassworks closed, due to reduced demand. In 1940 the Wingen factory was also forced to close, and was occupied by the Germans for the duration of World War II. Lalique himself stayed quietly in Paris throughout the Occupation, and died only two days after the unconditional surrender of the Germans, on May 9, 1945. Marc Lalique, already established as the company's chief administrator, undertook the renovation and reopening of the Wingen glassworks, and took on his father's role as chief designer. His major innovation was the introduction of a new raw material, containing twice as much lead oxide as Lalique's *demi-cristal*, which transformed the appearance of Lalique glass, giving it a clear, bright, modern style in keeping with a new age.

In a rare interview during the Paris Exposition, René Lalique was asked to define the methods and principles which underlay his design work. Describing design as a "perpetual task," he replied:

"I look at; I examine; a woman, a child, a bird in flight, whatever; a tree alive in the sunlight appears as fish beneath the water; suddenly the harmony of a shape, a gesture, a movement, becomes locked in my mind, combining with other ideas I have already acquired. Only when I have turned it all over and over in my head, does the idea, the oeuvre, ripen, and only then do I harvest it."

It is this cumulative process that links the goldsmith and the glassmaker, the creator both of unique Art Nouveau jewels and of mass-produced Art Deco vases, whose work spearheaded two great international exhibitions 25 years apart, and whose masterpieces are even more popular today.

Shown below is a selection of Lalique's vase and tableware designs. From left to right:

Ceylan vase, in opalescent and gray-stained glass with its decoration of paired parakeets.

Lièvres vase, a long-necked globular form in blue-stained glass with a band of leaping hares around the shoulder against a pattern of leafy branches.

Ceylan blue-stained vase.

Perruches bowl, featuring a band of parakeets set against a foliage background.

Graines vase, with a heavily beaded foot and flaring rim.

Actinia blue-stained vase with a rippling tentacle-like pattern.

SCENT BOTTLES & JEWELRY

Pages 26–27 and this page,
Clockwise from left:

Dans La Nuit, a blue glass bottle and stopper made for Worth for the perfume of the same name. The flattened bottle is spherical in shape and traces of a label survive on the side. The stopper is molded with stars. This design, of 1924, is known in several variations.

Worth, a clear and black enameled bottle and stopper, made for Worth, spherical in form and molded all over with low-relief stars. The stopper is molded with a "W." Again this design is known in several versions.

Je Reviens, a clear bottle made for Worth, flattened and spherical in form, with an applied gilt label, and with a disc-shaped stopper molded with a "W."

Le Lys, a clear, frosted and pink-stained bottle, in a flattened spherical shape, made for the perfume house of d'Orsay. The bottle is molded all over with a lily and foliage design and the stopper is a stylized version of the same flower. The applied gilt label and presentation case survive, an example of the new marketing concepts being applied to perfume.

28

Since the early days of civilization and certainly since classical times, perfume, the product of rare and expensive natural materials, was the preserve of a wealthy elite, as were the containers specially designed to hold it.

For centuries, craftsmen were inspired to create exquisite and delicate containers in glass and other materials to contain this precious product. Until the early 20th century, however, perfume bottles were created independently of individual scents and were decorative objects in their own right. Lalique's earliest efforts fall into this category. They were not intended for a particular perfume; their name reflected their design motif and so did not appear on the bottle; and no label was used. Examples in this style that can be seen in the following pages include *Amphitrite*, the bottle molded as a nautilus shell, the stopper in the form of a crouching nude (the sea nymph Amphitrite); *Quatre Cigales*, a tall square bottle with low-relief dragonflies molded on its shoulders; and *Paquerettes*, a tapering cylindrical bottle with a tiara-style stopper decorated with daisies. These would have been purchased empty from Lalique's company as a decorative item, either to be filled with perfume or to be displayed empty.

As a result of Lalique's relationship with the perfumier François Coty, however, the designer also began to create perfume bottles intended for a specific perfume and named for that perfume. With this apparently small change began a revolution in

Dans la Nuit, a clear, blue enameled, fully spherical bottle made for Worth and molded in low relief with scattered stars on a blue ground. The stopper is molded with the name of the perfume.

marketing, designed to help an ephemeral product achieve commercial success by providing each brand with a unique identity and appeal. Not just the bottle, but the name, the label and the box, all became a part of this packaging.

Thus *La Belle Saison*, created for the Houbigant perfume of the same name, could only be acquired when the perfume itself was purchased. The bottle was designed with a front medallion showing a young girl enjoying the scent of a flower, and with floral rays like shafts of sunshine radiating from this central motif. The medallion on the reverse was left smooth for the paper label, also designed by Lalique and bearing the name of the perfume.

From this the logical development was for Lalique to incorporate the name of the perfume into the bottle design itself, as can be seen in the perfume bottles: *Orée* with its name engraved on the square stopper; *Cyclamen*, designed for Coty with a central medallion bearing the name of the perfume engraved in the glass; and *Au Coeur des Calices*, also for Coty and bearing both the name of the perfume and the name of the perfumier.

Lalique continued to design perfume bottles throughout his long working life, and he also continued from time to time create jewelry items in glass. Two characteristic items are the *Naiade* pendant, featuring the sinuous sea-sprite which recurs in so much of Lalique's post-war design work, and the *Libellules* pendant, with its dragonfly theme.

30

Inner necklace: *Dahlias et Rondelles Plates*, in frosted and blue glass, and composed of pairs of floral beads in the form of dahlias, interspersed with flat disc-shaped beads. 37cm long. Lalique created several necklaces on floral themes in the 1920s, including fuchsia, daisy and lily-of-the valley. Designed for mass production, these are much simpler in conception than the ornate pieces he made in his goldsmithing and jewelry-working period. This example was first made in 1927.

Outer necklace: *Grosses Graines* necklace in blue glass, composed of oval beads molded in low relief as clusters of vines and berries, on a blue silk cord. Only three or four other long knotted designs in this style are known; most of Lalique's necklaces were designed choker-style.

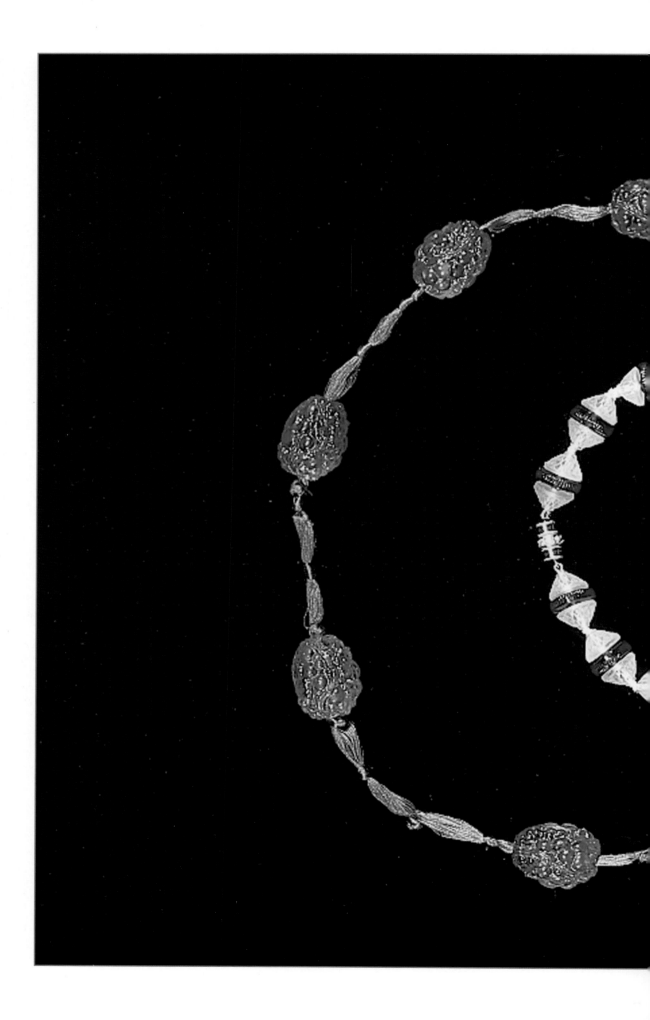

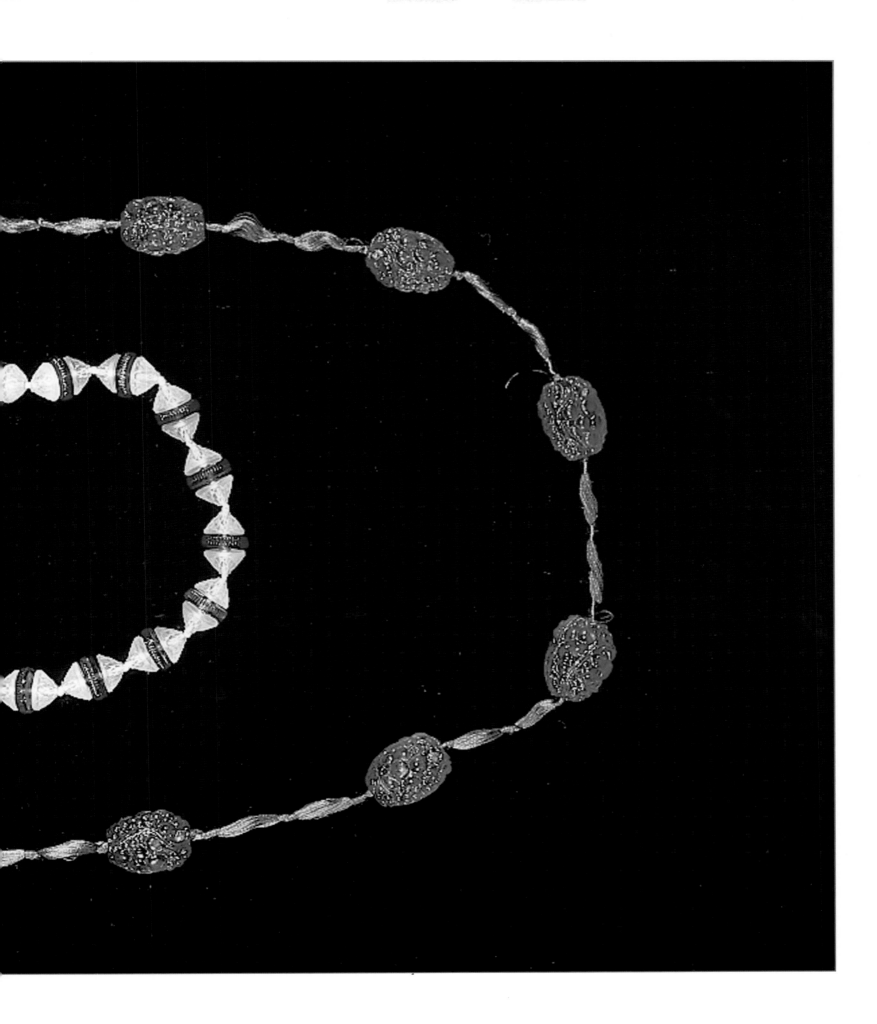

32

La Renommée d'Orsay perfume tester in clear, frosted and gray-stained glass, made for the perfume house of d'Orsay. Rectangular in shape, 22cm long, it contains five perfume wells, each with a flower-shaped stopper molded with the name of a perfume. The low-relief molding is in a design of interlaced briars, stamped with the name "D'Orsay." Created in 1922, it bears the molded mark "Lalique."

Ambre d'Orsay bottle in clear and frosted glass, made for the d'Orsay perfume house, cylindrical in shape, 13.7cm high, it has a gilt and gray metal band on the lower half which is cast in low relief with a frieze of dancing nymphs. The model was created around 1920 by Baccarat for the Lalique glassworks to produce, while the metal ring was designed by Lalique and is marked with the initials "R.L." The nymphs are unusual in their very purely classical conception; generally Lalique adapted such classical designs to the more plastic and sensuous style of his day (as in the paired statuettes *Moyenne Nue* and *Moyenne Voilée*), but these figures could have been lifted straight from a classical Greek frieze.

33

34

Tantot perfume bottle, in clear, frosted and blue-stained glass. Formed as a flattened oval with a fan-shape stopper, it is 14.5cm high and intaglio-molded all over with a design of interlacing flowerheads. It has a molded mark "R. Lalique," and is stenciled "France." Created in 1925, this is an example of the group of bottles made not for a particular perfume or perfume-house, but for general sale as a decorative item. The stylized flowerheads are characteristic of Art Deco designs of the period.

Capricornes clear, frosted and gray-stained bottle with a domed stopper. Both bottle and stopper are intaglio molded with an insect design. With an etched mark "Lalique," it is 8cm high. An early example of Lalique's press-molded perfume bottles created for open sale, this has a delicately curling and relatively lifelike design which recalls the fascination with insect life displayed in Lalique's jewelry designs of the 1890s.

Psyka, a clear and frosted bottle made for the perfume house Roger et Gallet, of flattened oval form with a flower-shaped stopper. The original model was created in about 1919. This example is still sealed, and still has the original paper labels bearing the name of the perfume and the perfume house. Unsigned, it is 9.5cm high.

Amphitrite frosted and sepia-stained bottle, molded as a nautilus shell, with a stopper in the form of a crouching female nude. It is engraved "R. Lalique France No. 514," molded "Lalique," and is 9cm high. Created in 1920 and made throughout the 1920s and 1930s, the realistically modeled nude previews the *Sirène* statuette which Lalique was to create some years later.

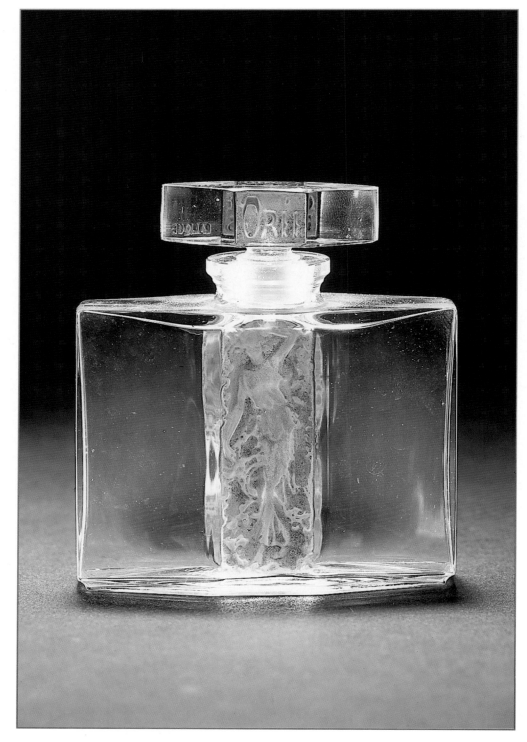

38

Orée, a clear, frosted and sepia-stained bottle made for Le Grand Magasin Claire from 1930. Rectangular in shape and with a lozenge-shaped stopper, the sides of the bottle are molded in low relief with a design of classically-styled nymphs within a foliage framework. The stopper is intaglio-molded with the name of the perfume and "Lalique."

39

Narkiss, a clear and frosted oval-shaped bottle and stopper made for Roger et Gallet and created in 1912. Each side of the 9.6cm high bottle is indented and molded as a single flowerhead, while the disc stopper is molded in low relief with two butterflies. There is an intaglio molded mark.

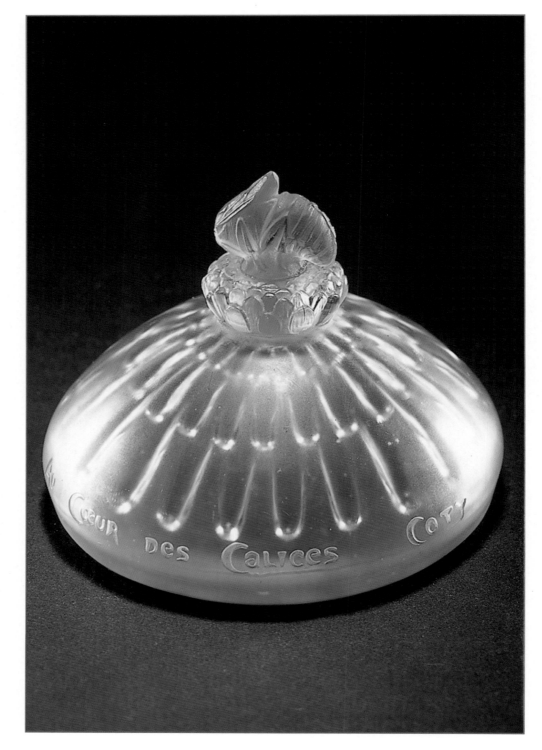

Au Coeur des Calices in frosted blue glass and modeled as a single stylized flowerhead with the stopper in the form of a wasp. It was made for Coty, the first perfume manufacturer with whom Lalique worked, and created in 1912. Intaglio-molded with the name of the perfume; the 6cm high bottle has the molded mark "Lalique."

41

À Coeur Joie, in clear and frosted glass, is 14.5cm high and molded in low relief with small flowers and with a clear heart-shaped central motif. The stopper is in the shape of a butterfly. The etched factory mark reads "Bottle Made By Lalique France." Made for Nina Ricci in 1942, this is a late creation and yet recalls the *Au Coeur des Calices* design of 30 years earlier, with its flower-ornamented body and insect-shaped stopper.

42

Hirondelles square bottle in clear, frosted and sepia-stained glass, molded in low relief with a design of swallows. Relief-molded "R. Lalique," it is 9cm high. The swallow motif is one of the commonest of all Lalique's bird and animal themes; he incorporated it as a car mascot, on clocks, a picture frame, vases and a cigarette box. This version was created in 1920.

Paquerettes, a clear and frosted bottle made for Roger et Gallet and created in 1919. The 8cm high bottle is undecorated, in a tapering cylindrical shape, and the tiara-style stopper is molded with a regular pattern of nodding, long-stemmed daisies. The molded mark "Lalique" is on the stopper. Lalique made a number of bottles with this style of tiara stopper, which give the impression of a bouquet of luxuriant, naturalistic flowers emerging from a vase. The bottles were often named after the design of the stopper, or *bouchon*, and some of Lalique's most dramatic and effective table lamps were designed on the same principle.

44

Poésie d'Orsay bottle, in frosted and sepia-stained glass and made for d'Orsay. It is shaped like a tapering cylinder, 14cm high, with a conical stopper which follows the line of the bottle. The bottle is molded in low relief with a frieze of dancing classical nymphs, set against a background of stars. Molded with the name of the perfume and with the mark "Lalique."

45

Flausa, in clear, frosted and sepia-stained glass, made for Roger et Gallet. A flattened ovoid in form, 11.5cm high, it is molded in low relief on each side with a single draped nymph, seated among blossom and holding out her hand. Intaglio-molded "Roger et Gallet," the stopper is molded "Lalique."

Pages 46–47: A selection of Lalique's vase and tableware designs. From left:

Ceylan vase, in opalescent and gray-stained glass with its decoration of paired parakeets.

Lièvres vase, a long-necked globular form in blue-stained glass with a band of leaping hares against a pattern of leafy branches.

Ceylan blue-stained vase.

Perruches bowl, with a band of parakeets set against foliage.

Graines vase, with a heavily beaded foot and flaring rim.

Actinia blue-stained vase with a rippling tentacle-like pattern.

Right: Three of Lalique's most popular and readily identifiable vases. Clockwise from top:

Dentelé, a clear and frosted vase, 18.5cm high, is molded in low relief with spine-like vertical ridges. Molded mark is "R. Lalique." Created in 1912, this design also exists as a perfume bottle.

Méduse is a frosted cylindrically-shaped vase, molded in low relief with undulating tentacles that curl upward toward the rim. The stencil mark is "R. Lalique." It is 16cm high. The decoration has a marine echo as suggested by the vase's name — the mythical Greek Medusa's hair grew in the form of sea-serpents.

Gui is a clear, frosted and gray-stained vase, ovoid in shape and densely molded in low relief with twining berry-bearing branches of mistletoe. It is intaglio-molded "R. Lalique," and is 16.5cm high. This design was created in 1920.

Perhaps the most consistently stunning of all Lalique's rich and varied output is the huge range of vases that he continued to create from his earliest days as a glassmaker to the very end of his prolific career, and which are today among the most sought after and collectable of all his products. Other contemporary glassmakers made decorative vessels, but no one matched Lalique for the sheer ingenuity of his technique and the range of his designs. The earliest examples, made before the turn of the century, used the *cire perdue* or lost wax technique, a laborious procedure which could be used only for one-of-a-kind pieces. These only rarely turn up in salerooms today and are hugely prized.

The majority of the vases (and other containers) that Lalique made from the 1920s onward are of mold-blown and press-molded glass, both techniques which permit mass production. A mold-blown vessel is created by blowing a bubble of glass, either by mouth or by automated means, into a mold, while a press-molded piece is made by shaping molten glass into a mold with a plunger. This second was the method introduced at Lalique's Wingen works in the 1920, and used to create both solid geometrical vessels in the Art Deco style and more delicate and ornately-ornamented vessels.

Before 1914, colored pieces are almost unknown, apart from a few pieces in a green similar to malachite or in black. Early experiments with color after the war tended to focus on a patinated effect, involving working on the surface of the vase, or on only a part of the decorative element, after it had been made. It was only from about 1925 onwards that the true production pieces were made available in a wide range of colors. *Gui* (mistletoe),

for example, created in 1920 and exploiting one of a range of natural motifs which had long been in Lalique's repertoire, was subsequently made in blue and green as well as Lalique's trademark opalescent. *Poissons* (fish) was made in blue, yellow, red and a delicately frosted version with sepia *patiné*; *Ronces* (brambles) in red, yellow, blue and sepia. These colors were created by adding a variety of chemicals to the base mix before the vessel was made, giving a much deeper and truer shade (depending on the quantities used) than the earlier technique. Copper oxide gave red; iron oxide yellow; manganese oxide a shade of violet/purple; cobalt oxide blue; and chrome oxide green. And all these shades could be varied in hue and intensity by combining them either with each other or with an opalescent base. This explains the diversity of colors that may be found within the same model range over a period of years, as the production process was slightly varied.

Almost all Lalique's work bears his signature in one form or another, the early goldsmithing pieced usually engraved "Lalique" or "R. Lalique" whereas the glass pieces may be wheel-engraved, impressed, etched, molded or acid-stamped. The various signatures can be clearly seen on the vases shown here and are detailed in the captions, but cannot easily be assigned to particular periods. Early engraved pieces, i.e. before about 1914, bear a fluid version of Lalique's signature; later engraved signatures often also bear the word "France." Wheel-cut signatures, with or without "France," appear on work from about 1925 through to the mid-1930s. Stencilled marks were made by sandblasting; molded marks were cast as an integral part of the object, and may appear in relief or in intaglio.

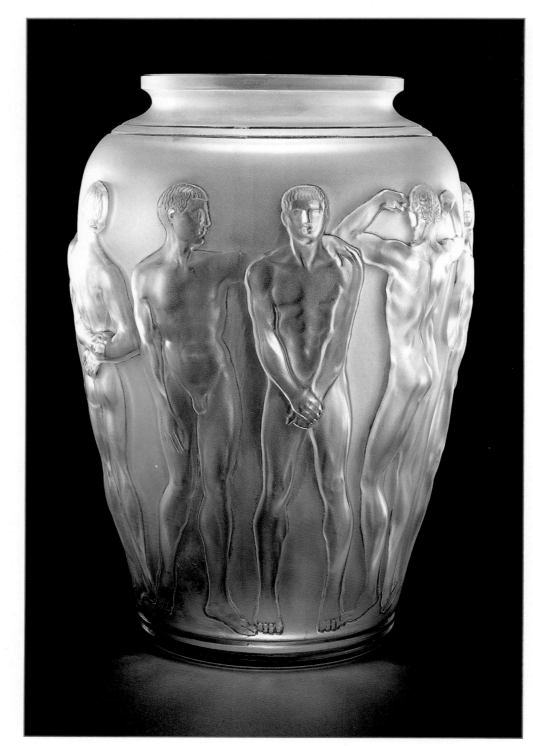

Palèstre, a tall — 40.5cm high — frosted and gray-stained vase molded with a frieze of nude male athletes in various gymnastic poses, is etched "R. Lalique." Most of Lalique's figural vases feature neoclassical female figures; this example (first made in 1928) and *Archers* are unusual in depicting males. A *palèstra* was the gymnasium where classical Greek athletes trained.

Right: *Naïades* vase, in clear satin-finished glass, designed as a cylindrical stem supporting a broad shallow bowl. The stem is deeply molded with a frieze of mermaids who support the bowl with their upraised arms and whose fishtails twine round each other to form the base of the vase. Between them sea-water ripples and their flowing hair is molded in similar ripples. Wheel-carved "R. Lalique France," it is 24.5cm high. This is an important example of Lalique's use of mermaids and sea-nymphs as a motif.

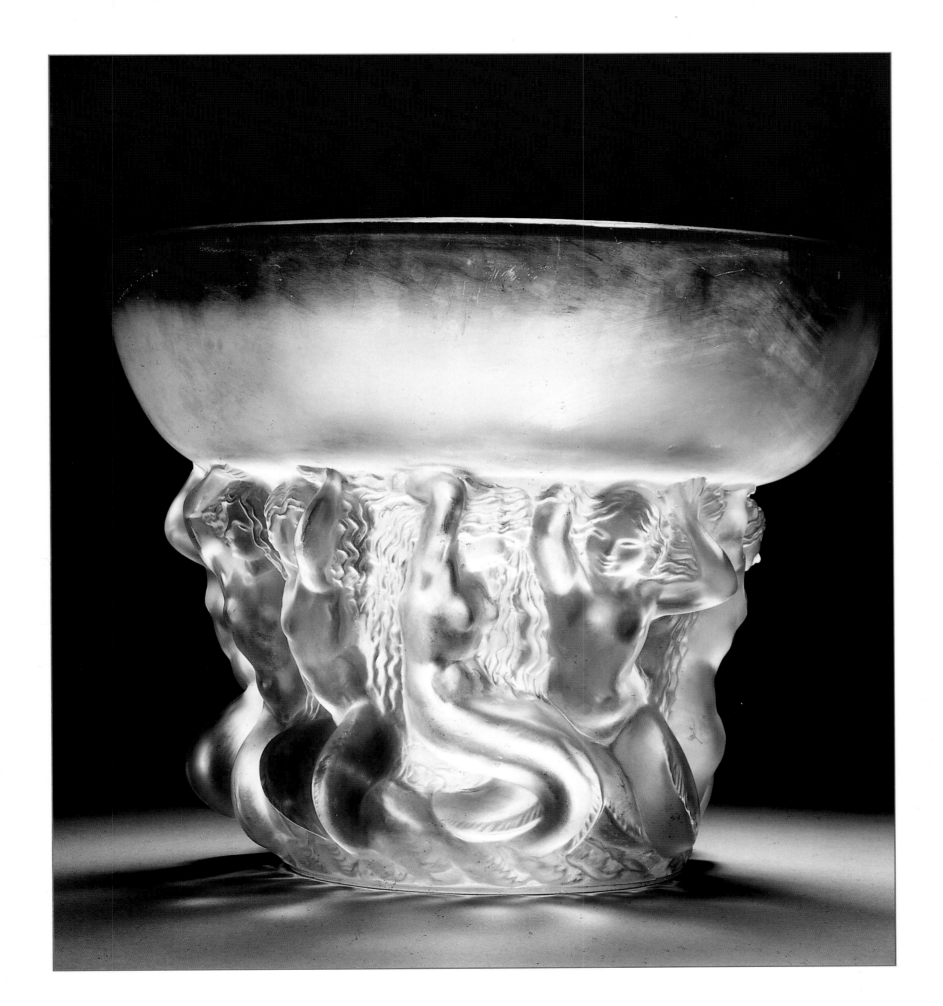

52

Penthièvre, a globular vase in blue glass with a flat circular collar rim, molded with four bands of geometrically stylized angel fish, is engraved "R. Lalique," and is 27cm high. The non-naturalistic design — as compared, for example, with the *Martigues* bowl — make this typical of Lalique's Art Deco work. It was created in 1928.

Languedoc, an emerald green, globular vase 22cm high with a short neck. The satin-finished glass is molded with bands of overlapping stylized leaves in a regular geometric design which again is characteristic of Art Deco style. It is engraved "R. Lalique France."

From left to right:

Ormeaux, clear and satin-finished amber-colored glass, in a globular shape with an everted rim. It is molded with a pattern of carefully veined leaves overlapping each other at a variety of angles, giving a looser and less formal effect than much of Lalique's geometric-style vegetation. Etched "R. Lalique France N 984," it is 17cm high.

Archers is a baluster-shaped vase in clear amber glass, molded on the lower half with figures of archers poised to unleash their arrows at the birds depicted in the upper half. Molded "R. Lalique," it is 26cm high. The twining bodies of both birds and men give this vase a dramatic quality that is lacking from most of Lalique's figural work. The model was created in 1921, early in the series of mass-produced vases, and is known in a wide range of colors including a rich red.

Formose, a globular vase in clear red glass, molded with a design of Chinese carp; the lamp fitting is a later addition. Molded "R. Lalique," it is diamond-engraved "R. Lalique France," and is 16.5cm high. The swimming fish are richly and texturally patterned and remarkably naturalistic compared with, for example, *Penthièvres*.

The cockerel car mascot is discussed on page 105.

54

56

Rampillons, a clear, frosted vase of tapering cylindrical form, is comparatively small. It is seen here in two versions, one in opalescent glass and one sepia-stained. It is molded in low relief with three tiers of large diamond shapes against a floral and leafy background. Both are wheel-engraved "R. Lalique France," and are 13cm high.

Oursin, a clear and frosted spherically shaped 18cm high vase with an everted rim, seen here also in a blue-stained version. It is shaped like a sea-urchin, with vertical spines and protruding nodules. The stencil mark is "R. Lalique," with "France" incised. This is an unusual design, in the sense that the motif is not purely decorative but dictates the form of the vase.

Avallon, a tapering cylindrical vase in clear, frosted glass, is seen here both in a purely opalescent and in a blue-stained opalescent version. It is molded in low relief with a richly naturalistic flora and fauna design of small birds exploring twisting berry-laden branches. Both are wheel engraved "R. Lalique France," and are 18cm high.

Laurier, a clear and frosted vase of cylindrical shape, is 17.5cm high and molded in low relief with laurel branches bearing leaves and berries. One is wheel-cut "R. Lalique France" and engraved "No. 947"; one is wheel-cut "R. Lalique France." The group of floral and foliate vase designs represents some of Lalique's richest and most varied work.

58

Above: *Saint-François* is a clear, frosted vase of tapering cylindrical form, shown both in opalescent and in blue-stained glass. It is molded in low relief with plump little birds which hang from leafy branches. Both examples have stencil mark "R. Lalique France," and are 18cm high. Created in 1930, this design belongs in the large group of vases based on naturalistic animal and bird themes.

Above Right: *Coquilles* is a cased opalescent and frosted design in a shouldered cylindrical shape, molded all over in low relief with large overlapping scallop shells. Both are engraved "R. Lalique France," and are 19cm high. The shell design is carefully observed, down to the fine vertical striations on each shell. This design was created in 1920, but the theme was one of Lalique's most popular, recurring on bowls, boxes, carafes and hanging lights.

Right: Two clear and frosted sharply tapering cylindrical vases, each molded in low relief with a decorative band at or near the base. *Piriac* (left), which bears traces of sepia staining, belongs in the group of marine decoration, with its charmingly naturalistic frieze of interlocking fish swimming above the four rippling waves which decorate the stem of the vase. Wheel engraved "R. Lalique France," it is 18.5cm high. *Pinsons* (right), sepia-stained, bears a band of birds interwoven with berried branches, reminiscent of the *Avallon* vase of the same period. Engraved "R. Lalique France No. 1038," it is 19cm high.

60

Damiers, a frosted and black-enameled vase, is shaped as a tapering cylinder with a foot. The acid-textured surface is enameled with a design of black squares that radiates from a central point toward the base of the 23cm high vase; it carries the stencil mark "R. Lalique." With its dramatic coloring and geometric design, this is one of Lalique's most powerful Art Deco designs, created in 1935.

Merles is a clear and frosted vase, very slightly tapering and paneled in form. The base is molded in high relief as two pairs of birds among berried branches — again the bird and berries theme, this time from 1931. Engraved "R. Lalique France," it is 28.5cm high.

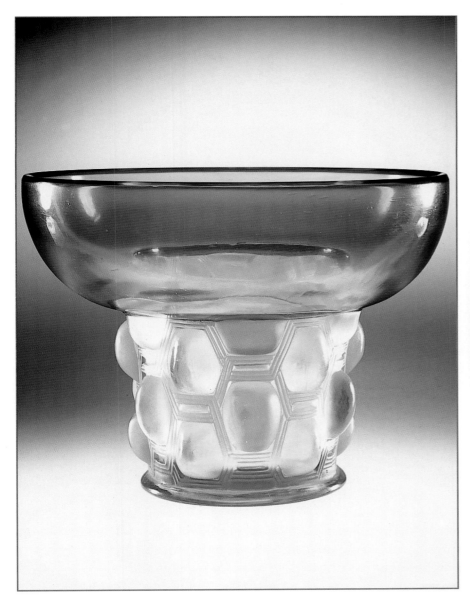

Beautreillis, an unusually shaped vase, is amber in color, 14.3cm high and cylindrical in form with a wide everted rim. The substantial stem is molded in low relief with a geometric design of raised ovals set in a linear framework. It is wheel-cut "R. Lalique France."

Ajaccio, a clear, frosted and sepia-stained vase of tapering cylindrical form, is molded in low relief with a ring of stars at the base, a band of seated gazelles immediately above, and a pattern of scattered stars on the body of the vase. Stencil mark is "R. Lalique France," and it is 20.5cm high. A particularly charming example of Lalique's use of animal themes, the gazelles are rudimentarily outlined; the power of the design lies in the curve of the animals' necks and the counter-curve of their horns.

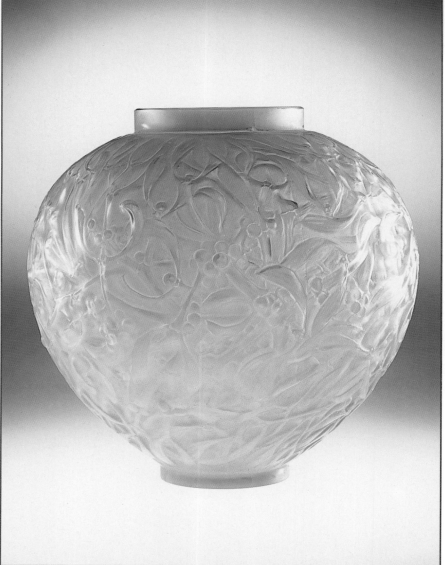

62

Comètes, a clear and frosted glass vase of flaring cylindrical form, is molded in low relief with comets which stand proud of the rim, while their geometrically linear tails decorate the side of the vase. Stencil mark is "R. Lalique France," and the vase is 28cm high.

Gui, a frosted amber vase of footed spherical form with a short neck, is molded all over in low relief with a twining pattern of mistletoe. It is intaglio-molded "R Lalique," and is 17cm high. Mistletoe is a recurring theme in all Lalique's decorative work, and this vase became one of his most popular items, reproduced both in opalescent glass and in a variety of colors. The model dates from 1920 and it remained in the catalog until 1947.

Yvelines is a clear, frosted and blue-stained vase, of swollen cylindrical form. Its two large protruding circular handles are each molded in low relief with a leaping deer among scrolling fern leaves which continue down the sides of the otherwise undecorated body. Wheel engraved "R. Lalique France" and engraved "No. 975," it is 20cm high.

Sauterelles, a clear, green and blue-stained vase is molded in low relief with a design of grasshoppers perching on curving blades of grass which criss-cross the body of the vase. Incised mark is "R. Lalique." It is 27.5cm high. First created as early as 1912, and therefore one of the earliest mass-produced designs, this vase displays a theme which appears in Lalique's work from his earliest ornate jewelry of the 1880s and 1890s. It was hugely popular and continued in production until 1947.

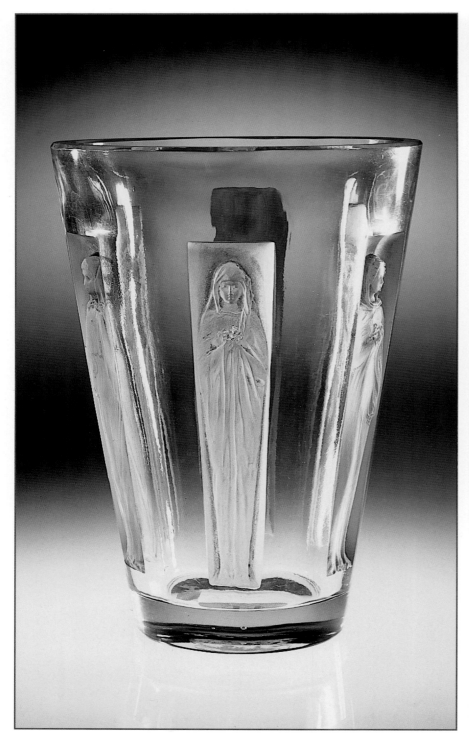

64

Goblet Six Figurines, a clear, frosted and blue-stained vase, is of tapering, cylindrical form, molded with six vertical rectangular panels, each bearing a veiled female figure in flowing robes, her hands clasped in an attitude of prayer. Engraved "R. Lalique," it is 19cm high. The design of the figures is reminiscent of the series of veiled figures, the *Statuettes de la Fontaine*, which Lalique created for the great fountain he designed for the 1925 Exposition.

Quatres Têtes Femmes et Raisins, is a clear, frosted and sepia-stained vase of tapering cylindrical form. Near the base it carries a decorative band, molded in low relief, showing four female masks set within berried foliage; the everted rim is decorated with grapes and vines. Stencil marked "R. Lalique France," height is 23cm. The female mask is drawn from the theatrical tradition of classical Greece, and reflects Lalique's preoccupation with classical decorative themes.

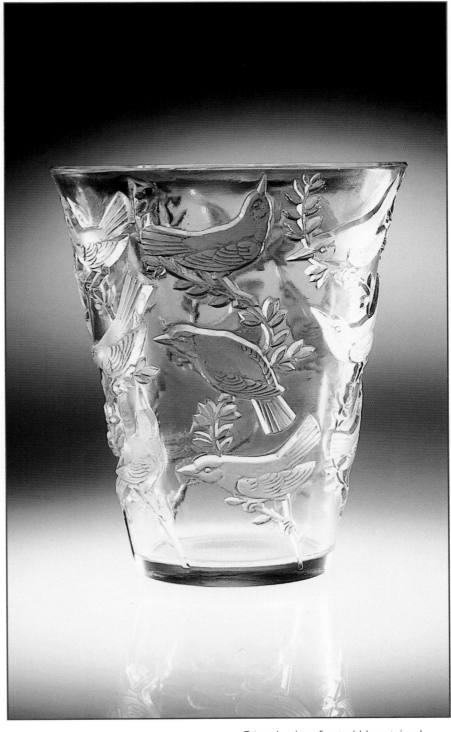

Bandes de Roses, a frosted and green-stained vase, is 23.5cm high. Its shoulder-tapering, cylindrical shape is intaglio-molded with eight narrow vertical bands bearing small, stylized roses. It is intaglio-molded "Lalique." First created in 1919, this design was produced in clear as well as matt and polished glass.

Grives, in clear, frosted blue-stained glass, is a tapering, cylindrical vase, molded all over in low relief with a pattern of birds perched on leafy branches. Stencil mark is "R. Lalique •France," and it is 17.5cm high. A late contribution to Lalique's bird vase designs, this was created in 1938, just before the outbreak of World War II brought production at Wingen to a halt.

Paquerettes, a frosted and opalescent vase of cylindrical form, is molded all over in low relief with a design of daisies and foliage. It carries the stencil mark "R. Lalique France," and is 18cm high. The daisy motif is one that occurs regularly in Lalique's later work.

Martin-Pêcheurs, a clear and frosted vase of swollen cylindrical form with a short rim, is molded all over with a stylized design of kingfishers perched on interlaced leafy branches. Stencil mark is "R. Lalique," and it is 24.5cm high.

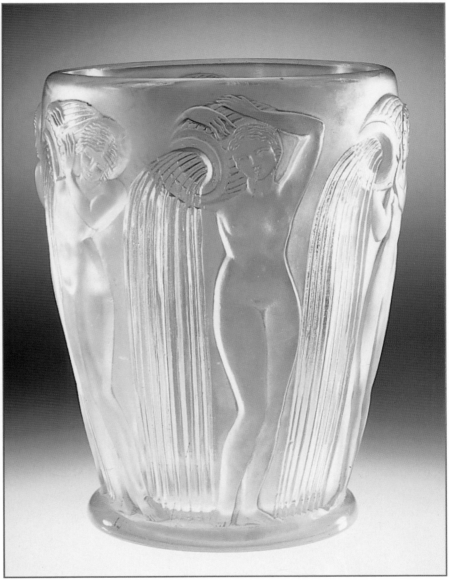

Périgord is a cased opalescent vase, squat and bulbous in form, with protruding ridges. Engraved "R. Lalique France," it is 14cm high.

Danaïdes, a clear, frosted and opalescent vase, of tapering cylindrical shape, is molded all over in low relief with a frieze of classical female nudes, bearing huge urns on their shoulders from which they pour stylized streams of water. Wheel-engraved "R. Lalique France" and engraved "No. 972," it is 18.3cm high. One of the most important and popular of Lalique's figural vases, this was first created in 1926, and manufactured in both colored and smoked glass as well as the opalescent version seen here.

Soucis, an opalescent glass vase, bulbous in form with an everted rim and foot, is molded in low relief with a pattern of dahlia-like flowerheads and foliage. The stencil mark is "R. Lalique," and it is 17.5cm high.

Ceylan, a clear, frosted, opalescent and blue-stained vase, cylindrical in shape and with an everted rim, is molded in low relief with loving pairs of parakeets perched on branches that curve up from the foot of the vase. Wheel-cut "R. Lalique France" and engraved "No. 905," it is 24cm high. These lovebirds are among the most naturalistic and charming of all Lalique's bird designs.

Pivoines, a clear, frosted and opalescent vase of tapering cylindrical form, molded in low relief with scattered flowerbuds. Stencil-marked is "R. Lalique France," and it is 17cm high. A late creation, first seen in 1937, this design does not figure in the catalogs and was not made after 1947.

Margaret is a clear, frosted and blue-stained vase, rectangular in shape, with two rectangular handles each molded in low relief with small birds among berried branches. The molded mark is "R. Lalique" and "France" is wheel-cut. It is 24cm high. An unusually uncompromising shape, but with realistically observed birds, this design was created in 1929 and is a particularly rare example of Lalique's work.

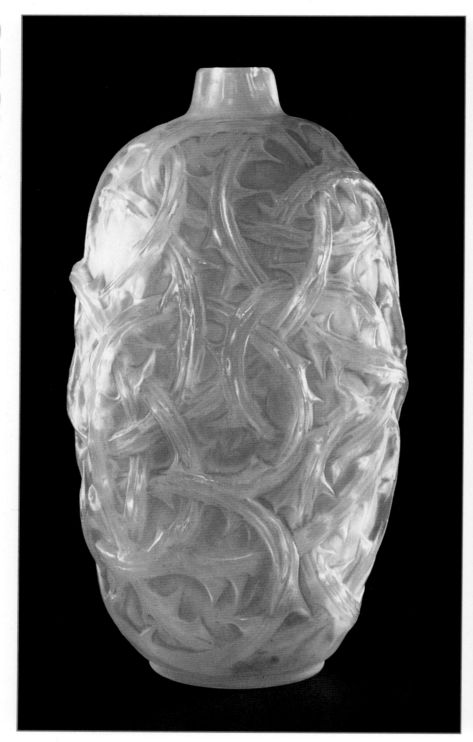

Ronces, an ovoid vase in opalescent glass stained gray, is molded all over in low relief with a pattern of inter-lacing briars. Wheel-engraved "R. Lalique France No. 946," it is 23cm high. First created in 1921 and remaining in the Lalique company catalogs until 1947, this vase nonetheless recalls Lalique's earlier Art Nouveau designs, with its thickly fleshy twining briar stems.

Bacchantes vase, in frosted and opalescent glass, molded in low relief with a frieze of classical nymphs, it bears the molded mark "R. Lalique" and wheel-cut "France." 24cm high, it is an important example of Lalique's figurative vase work, with its rounded, muscular, gracefully dancing female nudes and sculptural background, making a striking contrast with the more stylized *Danaïdes* vase.

Poissons is a cased spherically-shaped vase with short neck and everted rim, in red glass. It is molded all over in low relief with a design of scaly fish, and engraved "R. Lalique France." 23.5cm high, this was a particularly popular example of Lalique's fish-design vases, and was made in vivid blue and yellow as well as the red shown here. The design, with its aggressive, carefully observed bull-headed fish, was first created in 1921, quite early in Lalique's mass-production work, and is reminiscent of some of his unique *cire perdue* pieces.

Bresse, a footed spherical vase in vivid peppermint green, is intaglio-molded in low relief with a design of stylized cockerels, whose curving tail feathers form an interlocking symmetrical pattern over the body of the vase. Stencil mark is "R. Lalique France"; it is 10cm high.

72

Tournesols, an ovoid vase with everted rim, in electric blue glass, is molded in low relief with a design of interlocking sunflowers, their centers bulbously protruding from the body of the glass. Engraved "R. Lalique France No. 1007," it is 11.5cm high.

Charmilles, a large frosted and sepia-stained vase, ovoid in form with an everted rim, is molded all over with a pattern of skeletal leaves which appear to emerge from the body of the vase. Incised "R. Lalique France," it is 35.5cm high.

Soustons vase, in opaque glass with enameled decoration. The whole design is conceived as a single vegetal or artichoke shape, with overlapping stylized leaves. It was first made in 1935.

Cérises vase, one of a number of variations on the theme of small fruit, all designed around 1930. This has a convex base molded with a relief design of cherries and leaves, with a plain flaring body.

Oran, a particularly popular vase, first made in 1927 and which continued in the catalogs until after Lalique's death. In the characteristic press-molded open shape, it is decorated with large stylized dahlia heads in low relief.

Pages 76–77: Here are displayed some of Lalique's most characteristic and successful tableware designs, all featuring familiar vegetal and marine ornamentation. Clockwise from bottom left:

Paquerettes champagne glass and lunch plate, both in clear, frosted and blue-stained glass and decorated with a band of stylized and regular daisy heads. Both bear the stencil mark "R. Lalique France." The plate is one of a set of three of different sizes, also with matching bowl, and the glass one of a set of seven with matching carafe and water jug.

Pissenlit handbowl and matching plate, in clear, frosted and sepia-stained glass, molded on the underside with a pattern of stylized dandelion leaves. Molded marks "R. Lalique" engraved and wheel-cut "France."

Coquilles bowl, in clear, frosted and opalescent glass, molded in low relief with delicately patterned overlapping scallop shells, also used on a vase design.

Right: *Fleur* fingerbowl, in clear, frosted, gray and sepia-stained glass, molded in low relief as a large flowerhead whose petals lap up the side of the bowl. An early creation, this design dates from 1912 and its naturalistic irregularity, very different from the equally striking but rigidly formal *Coquilles*, reflects a continuing Art Nouveau influence in Lalique's work at that point.

78

While vases are among the most highly regarded of Lalique's post-war creations, the largest category of commercial production from the Wingen factory was devoted to tableware. In response to a growing demand for reasonably-priced, well-designed, non-crystal pieces, Lalique turned his creative skills to the practical requirements of serving a meal, and at once found an eager and appreciative market. The critic Gabriel Mourey spoke for many of his contemporaries when he wrote:

"What is strangely amazing is that Lalique manages to create, after so many others, a table set and yet remain original. The reason is that he always sticks to reason and logic and abhors eccentricity; that he always clings to nature, as far as it is possible to do so — thanks to the assembling of the two techniques — of cut glass and cast glass, there is practically no liberty that is forbidden to him; thus for instance, he has succeeded in incorporating to the foot of a wineglass of cut crystal tiny figures made of cast glass which give to the object a supplementary charm."

The first carafes and goblets, such as the *Deux Danseuses* carafe, with its characteristically bulbous body and tall tapering neck, were created before 1915, but the vast bulk of Lalique's work in this field dates from the 1920s and 1930s and consists of complete sets of tableware bearing a range of decorative motifs drawn from the familiar repertoire. The *Paquerettes* set, for instance, features the

daisy decoration also found on the vase of the same name; the plate and champagne glass are illustrated on the previous page. Other familiar themes reappear on the *Poissons* (fish), *Ormeaux* (elmleaf) and *Coquilles* (shell) table sets. Motifs used for complete table sets tended to be less daring than those used for vases — the pieces did after all have to be functional. The most regularly used decorative patterns were floral and animal, but in the 1930s some more purely geometric designs appear, as in the *Unawihr* set.

Bowls could be designed as stand-alone pieces, however, and some of these display a more radical approach to design, such as the *Chiens no. 1* bowl from 1921, with its sinuous and vigorous greyhounds against a radiating thistle motif, or the *Roscoff* bowl, its underside molded with a design of random bubbles and emerging fish.

Wine glasses too, as indicated by Mourey, could be given a characterful treatment, such as the four frogs which crouch at the base of the *Quatre Grenouilles* glass from 1912. More typical of the mass-production line was the *Monogramme* glass service, created in 1924 and consisting of carafe, plus glasses for water, burgundy, claret, champagne, liqueurs and madeira respectively, or the *Unawihr* service from 1926, of carafe, jug, and glasses for water, claret, madeira, champagne and liqueurs.

The catalog *raisonné* of Lalique's work includes some 70 different designs for complete sets of this kind, some indicator of the comfortable lifestyle for which Lalique was catering.

79

Above: *Pouilly*, a clear, frosted and green-stained finger-bowl, first created in 1933. It is molded at the base in low relief with a band of stylized fish.

Right: Various Lalique glasses. From the front:

Six *Saint-Nabor* madeira glasses, designed in 1926 as a set also including water, claret and champagne glasses, a carafe and a water jug. The bowl is of clear glass, the stem is black enameled with a stylized loop design.

One *Unawihr* madeira glass, with a clear bowl and black-enameled stem, with a pattern of black ridges.

Three *Graines* tumblers in clear and frosted glass.

Two *Dohrnach* clear and frosted claret glasses, their slightly bulbous cylindrical stems molded with stars.

Deux danseuses carafe, in clear and frosted glass with a tapering neck and a flattened spherical body. The central circular panel is decorated with two naked nymphs capering among streams of floral garlands. This is an early example of Lalique's tableware, first created in 1912, and the nymphs are shown in a sinuous Art Nouveau style.

Part of a *Vouvray* service, comprising in total decanter, six each of water glasses, burgundy glasses, claret glasses, liqueur glasses, madeira glasses, and five champagne glasses. The footed conical glasses are decorated with regularly spaced serrated bands in a geometrical style characteristic of Lalique's work in the 1930s.

Hesperides jug and tumbler set, first made in 1931 and decorated with stylized fern leaves. The Garden of the Hesperides was a legendary place in Greek myth where the apples of youth were supposed to grow.

A selection of carafes. Clockwise from left:

Vouvray, decorated with serrated conical banding on clear glass.

Saint-Nabor (matching madeira glasses are shown on p. 80).

Unawihr carafe, in clear glass with an enameled stopper molded in low relief with a pattern of a low ridges.

Phalsbourg carafe, in clear glass with decorative stopper.

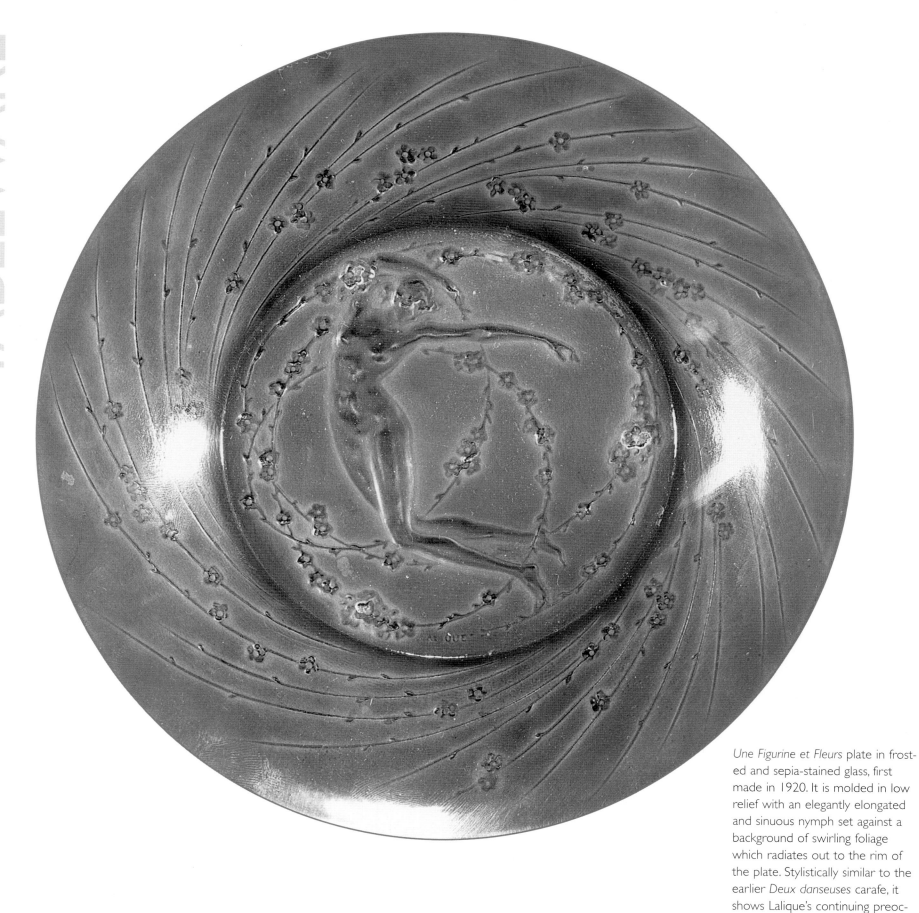

Une Figurine et Fleurs plate in frosted and sepia-stained glass, first made in 1920. It is molded in low relief with an elegantly elongated and sinuous nymph set against a background of swirling foliage which radiates out to the rim of the plate. Stylistically similar to the earlier *Deux danseuses* carafe, it shows Lalique's continuing preoccupation with classical Greek motifs.

This selection of Lalique's tableware shows (clockwise from top left):

Campanules dish, in clear and opalescent glass, molded with a pattern of graduated bands of tulips. Stencil mark "R. Lalique France."

Muguet, a shallow dish in clear and frosted glass, molded with a pattern of lily of the valley and foliage. Stencil mark "R. Lalique France." A post-World War II frosted tray, its sides molded in low relief with a raffia design.

Rosace, a shallow bowl in blue glass with three short feet. First made in 1930, it is molded with a geometrical design of slightly curvaceous graduated triangles. Stencil mark "R. Lalique France."

Ormeaux No. 1, a clear, frosted and green-stained plate, part of a service first created in 1931. It is molded in a design of stylized leaves arranged in concentric circles. Stencil mark "R. Lalique France."

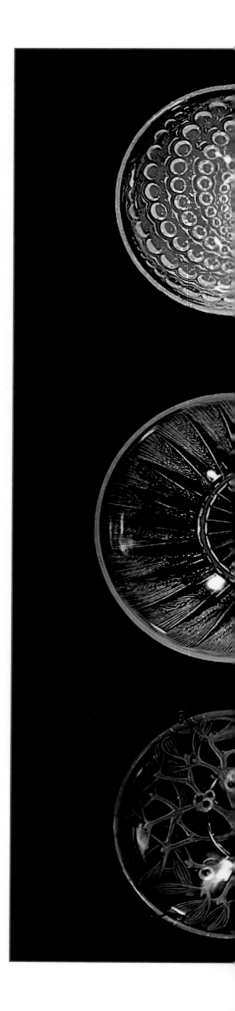

88

A selection of some of Lalique's most stunning bowl designs. Right, from left to right and top to bottom:

Volutes, in clear and opalescent glass with a spiraling bubble design.

Oursins, in the shape of a sea-urchin.

Chicorée No. 1, a curvaceously serrated leaf design.

Volubilis, two examples, both in opalescent glass with a design of three poppy-like star-shaped flowerheads.

Epis No. 1, in clear glass with a pattern of ears of corn.

Plumes de paon, in clear and opalescent glass with a design of overlapping peacock feathers.

Poissons No. 1, in clear glass, molded with a pattern of spiraling, interlinked fish.

Gui No.5 bowl, in clear, frosted and sepia-stained glass and molded with a pattern of mistletoe.

Actinia, in opalescent glass and with a spiraling pattern of wavering, radiating ferns.

Coquilles No. 2, a scallop shell pattern.

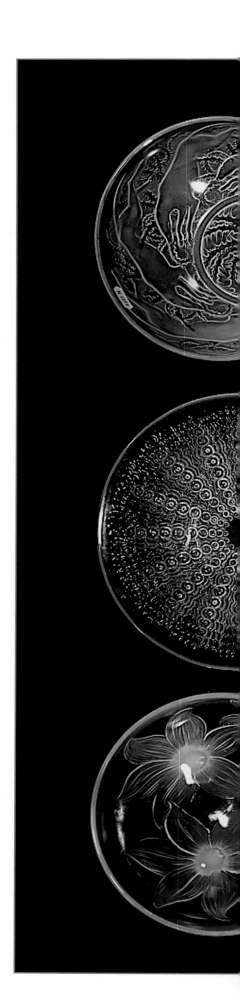

A selection of plates, dishes and bowls. Right, from left to right and top to bottom:

Chiens No. 1, a clear, frosted and opalescent bowl, decorated with a frieze of sinuous bounding greyhounds, set against a foliate background of prickly acanthus-like leaves radiating out from a central point.

Poissons No. 2 plate in clear and opalescent glass, molded with a design of spiraling fish.

Plumes de paon bowl, in clear opalescent glass with a design of overlapping peacock feathers.

Asters clear and opalescent glass bowl with a design of regularly-placed flowerheads.

Oursins No. 2 plate, in clear and opalescent glass, molded in low relief with a sea-urchin-like pattern of radiating nodules.

Pissenlit No. 1 dish in clear and frosted glass, first made in 1921 and molded with a pattern of dandelion leaves.

Vases No. 1 plate, a rare design of stylized Greek vases against a leaf and flower background.

Lys, a clear, frosted and opalescent bowl first made in 1924, molded in low relief with four loosely designed and open flowerheads, their stalks forming the bowl's four feet.

Chicorée No. 1 bowl in opalescent glass, molded with a low-relief pattern of spiraling acanthus leaves. The acanthus was a standard motif in Greek classical sculpture, used for instance in the decoration of of column capitals.

Lys bowl in clear, frosted and opalescent glass with flowerhead motif.

Volutes bowl, in clear and opalescent glass in a design of swirling bubbles.

92

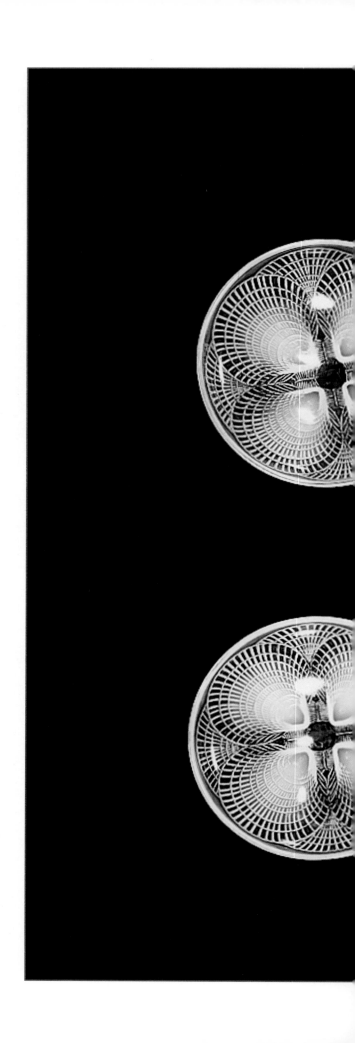

Right: (from left) A selection of Lalique's *Coquilles* tableware set, decorated with a scallop shell pattern, which includes a large and three small bowls and two plates.

Chiens No. 1 bowl, in clear, frosted and sepia-stained glass, with a band of leaping hounds decorating the exterior.

Ondines clear and opalescent bowl, with a design of five spiraling sea sprites.

This selection of bowls and dishes features Lalique's use of animal and vegetal motifs on his tableware services. Right, from left to right, top to bottom:

Chataignier, a clear and frosted bowl first made in 1933, here seen in a post-World War II version, featuring a radiating pattern of dandelion leaves.

Gazelles dish in smoked glass with a wide overhanging rim, which is decorated with three carefully delineated and naturalistic gazelles against a background of more rigidly designed leafy garlands.

Marguerites, a clear, frosted and blue-stained bowl, with a wide rim which is decorated with a band of overlapping daisy flowerheads.

This *Chataignier* bowl is in a style created in the 1930s.

Poissons No. 1 shallow bowl, in clear and opalescent glass, with a design of slender fish spiraling in toward the center, first created in 1921.

Algues bowl in opalescent glass with a design of spiraling and formalized foliage.

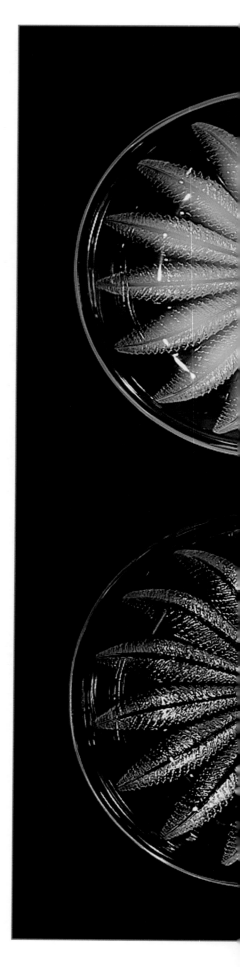

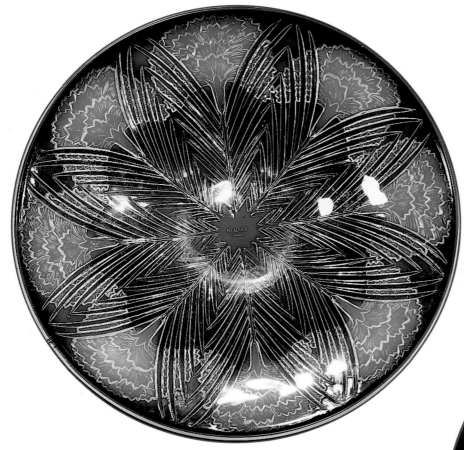

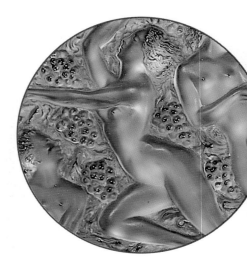

96

Above: *Oeillets*, a large shallow bowl in clear and opalescent glass, with a superbly formalized design of thistle heads and foliage. First made in 1932, this was also produced in colored glass.

Above and Top: *Côte d'Or* plate, also known as *Trois Figurines et Raisins* and made in clear and frosted glass. The center is molded in low relief with three naked nymphs whose curvaceous dancing shapes are carefully adapted to the shape of the plate. The background is filled in with grapes and vines, and the rim is decorated with regularly spaced bunches of grapes. The design dates from 1943, right at the end of Lalique's life, and yet harks back to some of his earliest classicizing designs.

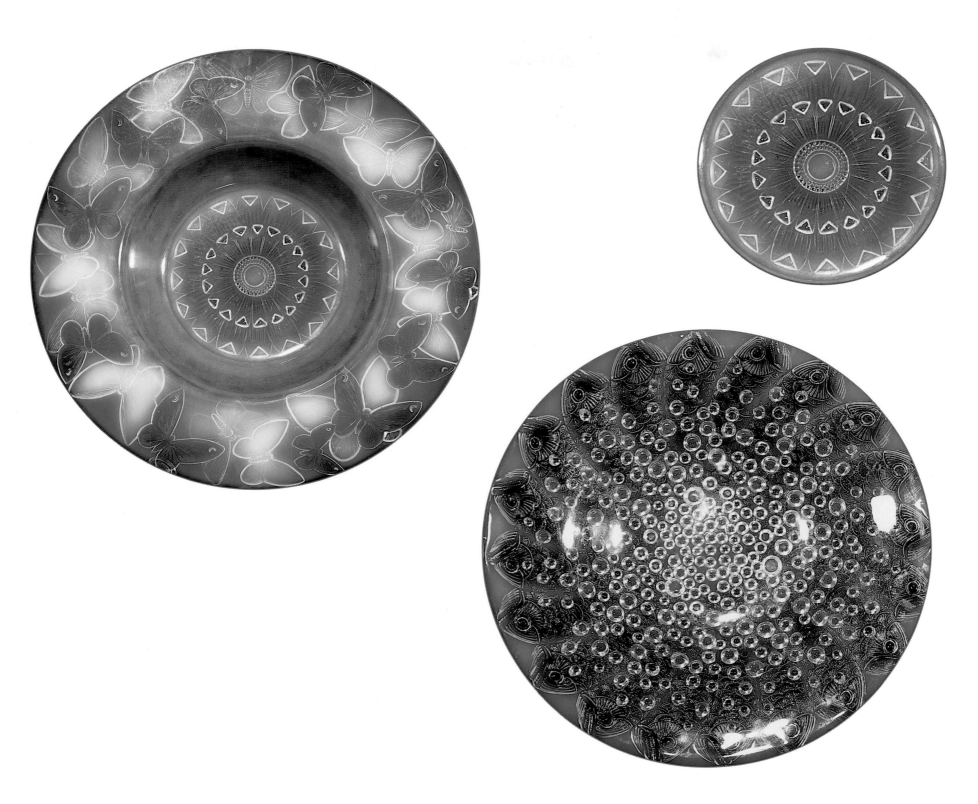

Above and Top Right: *Phalènes* bowl, in clear, frosted, opalescent and blue-stained glass, first made in 1929. Conceived in three decorative bands, the center consists of a single very stylized flowerhead, surrounded with a plain band, and the rim is decorated with irregularly overlapping butterflies.

Above: *Roscoff* bowl, one of Lalique's most effective designs, with its charming formalized fishheads which seem to emerge round the rim from the central spiral of bubbles. First created by Lalique in 1932.

98

Above and Top Right: *Martigues*, in frosted and opalescent glass, an early example of Lalique's use of the fish motif, dating from 1920. It makes an interesting comparison with the more geometrical *Roscoff*. Here the fish are conceived in the round and seen in energetic motion.

Above and Left: *Calypso* bowl in clear, frosted and opalescent glass. The wide everted rim is molded with a design of five mermaids. More formalized and less voluptuous than those on the *Ondines* service, their hair and tails shade off into ripples of water. Stencil mark "R. Lalique."

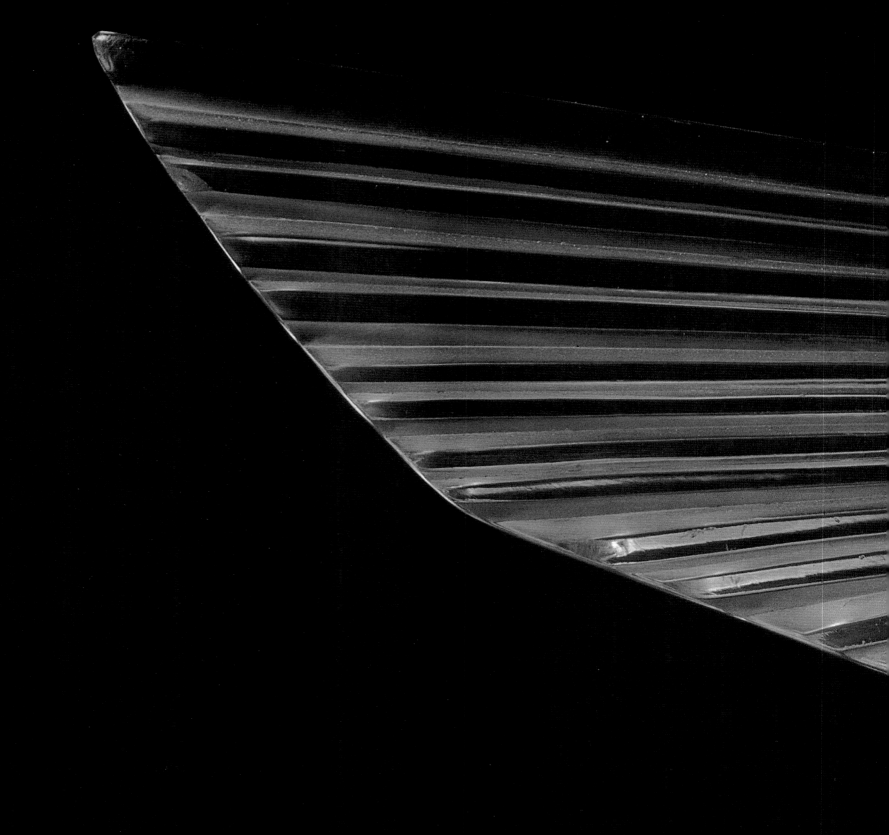

Pages 100-102: *Victoire* car mascot, one of Lalique's most famous and familiar creations, conceived in a characteristically Art Deco spirit, with linear features and stylized flowing hair.

The three Lalique statuettes below are: *Clos Sainte-Odile*, (left) a Lalique brown-stained statuette with dish (possibly a variation on the very similar *Source de la Fontaine* ashtray), press-molded as a draped figure holding a book to her chest, the base molded with the words "Clos Sainte-Odile." This is mounted on a shallow circular clear glass dish, with an

engraved signature "R. Lalique France." 10.1cm high.

Sirène statuette (see right)

Drapée (right), an opalescent statuette in the form of a female nude holding drapery which falls in folds round her feet, on a circular base. Engraved signature "R. Lalique." 6.5cm high.

Lalique's car mascots are among his most distinctive and valued creations, and almost all date from a six-year period between 1925 and 1932, coinciding with a period of huge enthusiasm for that still-novel creation, the automobile. It was an Englishman, Lord Montagu of Beaulieu, who introduced the idea of the car mascot in the 1890s, when he placed a St. Christopher statuette on the bonnet of his Daimler, while in 1911 Rolls-Royce launched their "Spirit of Ecstasy" figure which still adorns their cars today. By the 1920s car manufacturers were offering mascots as a way of personalizing a car, and in 1925 Citroen had the bright idea of commissioning Lalique to create a mascot design.

This was the *Faucon* mascot, and Lalique went on to create a series of mascots modeled on bird and animal designs. These included the familiar *Cinq Chevaux* designed for the Citroen car of that name (the model was produced only days later than the *Faucon* — August 20, 1925, as against August 6, some indicator of the sheer creative ferment in which Lalique worked). Others were the *Tête de l'Aigle* (eagle's head) mascot, a motif also used for seals and paperweights; the glorious *Tête de Paon* (peacock's head), the charming *Perche* (perch) and, reverting to Lalique's penchant for the slightly macabre, the *Grenouille* (frog). These were not only produced in the full range of colors which Lalique had developed in glass manufacturing, but could also be illuminated in an even wider variety of hues by using interchangeable light filters.

Another regular subject for car mascots is the female nude, such as *Chrysis*, a late creation of 1931 and named after the mythical Greek hero Agamemnon's lover, and *Sirène*. Lalique had

begun to experiment with the theme of the nude as early as the first decade of the 20th century, working in the laborious and beautiful *cire perdue* method, and the influence of classical Greek sculpture (as hinted at by Chrysis' name) is clear. The piece *Figurine avec Guirlande de Fruits* shown on page 114 dates from 1912 and is a press-molded version of an original model that would have been created in *cire perdue*. *Cire perdue* statuettes are very rare and commensurately valuable — there was great excitement when a wholly unknown and uncataloged, but unmistakably Lalique, statuette of a female nude covered in tendrils was discovered in 1987 — and even the press-molded 1912 version is relatively unusual.

The majority of surviving statuettes are production models from the 1920s and 1930s. These include the matched pair, *Moyenne Voilée* and *Moyenne Nue*, each of them sensuously semi-clothed in figure-revealing classical draperies, and the more classically hieratic *Voilée Mains Jointes* (here adapted into a table lamp and included on page 141 in the section on Lighting). More firmly in the Art Deco style are the two best-known of Lalique's female figures, *Suzanne* (also known as *Suzanne au bain* and apparently loosely based on the biblical story of Susannah and the Elders) and *Thaïs*. These two sinuous sensual nudes both appear to be stepping self-consciously from the bath or bed, trailing behind them from outstretched arms a rippling sheet of drapery, exquisitely molded in translucent glass. *Thaïs*, the more erotic and abandoned of the two, is also considerably rarer, though both pieces continued to be made at Wingen for more than ten years from 1925.

Sirène statuette in opalescent satin-finished glass, molded as a crouching mermaid with her head on one side, on a circular base. Engraved signature "R. Lalique France No. 831." 20 cm high.

Suzanne (sometimes also called *Suzanne au bain*) statuette, here in amber glass, also available in other colors and in opalescent glass, molded as a female nude with drapery falling in translucent folds from her outstretched arms and creating an almost square composition on a flared plinth. Molded signature "R. Lalique." 23cm high. Among the best-known and most popular of all Lalique's pieces, this was first created in 1925 and stayed in the catalog until 1937. A sketch design for the piece dates from 1922 and suggests it was also made in a *cire perdue* version, and it can also be found adapted as a light fitting.

Coq nain car mascot in dark gray clear and satin-finished glass, molded as a full-length cockerel proudly displaying its tail feathers. Partly molded signature "R. Lalique," engraved "France no.1135." 20cm high. Created in 1928, this model with its angularly stylized feathers was particularly popular, and was also available in opalescent glass. The same design can be found as a paperweight.

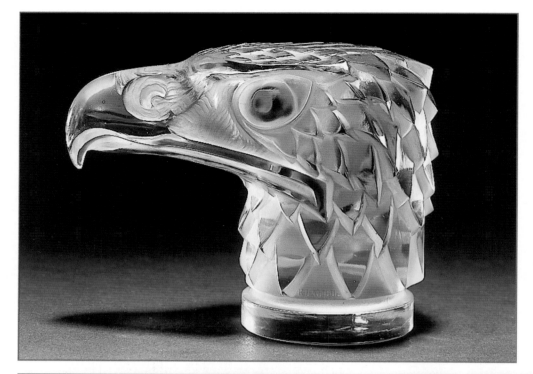

Above Right: *Tête de l'Aigle* car mascot, in clear and frosted glass, modeled as an eagle's head. Molded mark "R. Lalique France." 11cm high. This powerful and uncompromising image with its stylized feathers, fierce gaze and threatening beak was also made in a variety of colors, including a rare and beautiful amethyst blue. The design, first created in 1928, was also used for a seal and for book-ends, and may have provided the template for the eagle-head mas-cot adopted by Hitler's Third Reich.

Right: A pair of *Tête de coq* book-ends in clear and frosted glass, each modeled as a cockerel's head on a shaped rectangular cream onyx stand, and based on the car mascot design of the same name which was created in 1928. Intaglio-molded "R. Lalique France." 19.5cm high. The neck feathers and comb are stylized in the man-ner of the eagle-head mascot.

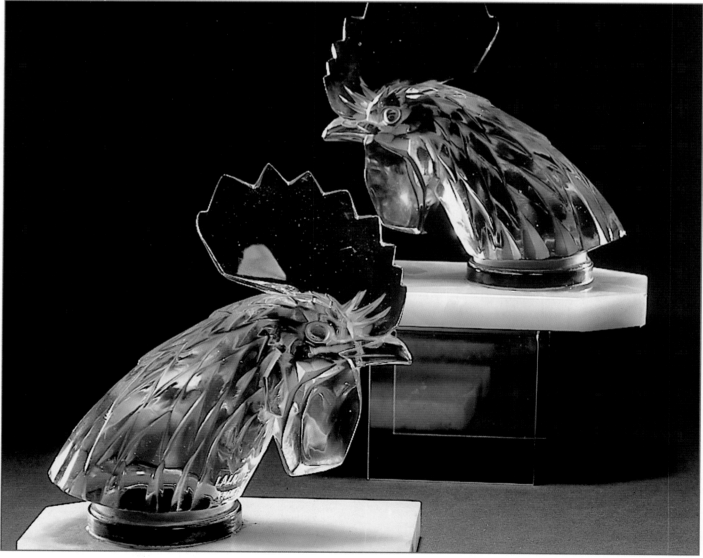

Above Left: *Tête de l'Epervier* car mascot, in topaz-colored clear and frosted glass, modeled as the head of a sparrowhawk. Molded mark "Lalique France No.1157." 6.5cm high. This is designed in a more flowing and rounded style than the other two bird's head mascots, and is reminiscent of images of the Egyptian falcon-headed god Horus.

Left: *Perche* car mascot, in opalescent glass, molded in the form of a perch, in its original Breves Gallery chrome mount. Wheel-cut mark "R. Lalique France," molded mark "R. Lalique." 9cm high. One of the more charming of Lalique's car mascots, this was first created in 1929 and was also available in clear and in amber glass, the former still made today. The delicate molding of the scales is particularly lifelike and impressive when compared with the stylized rendition of feathers on the bird's head mascots.

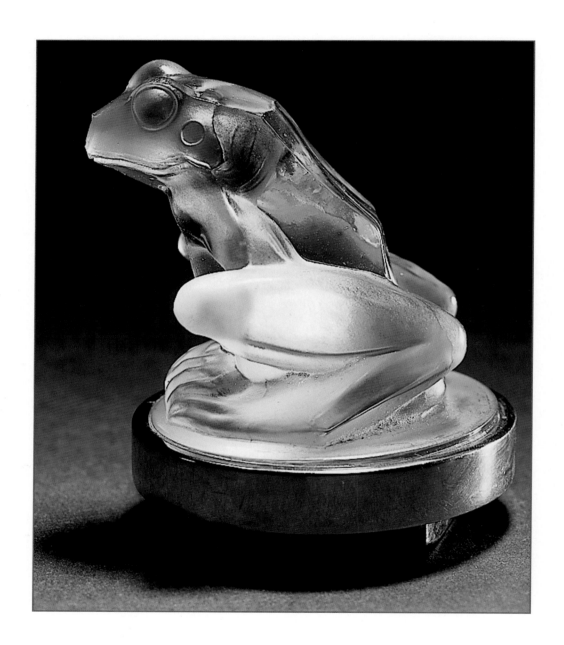

Grenouille car mascot in clear and frosted glass, molded in the shape of a squatting frog and fitted in a chrome metal mount with a green reflector. Molded mark "R. Lalique." 13.5cm high. Now very rare, this is realistically modeled in the round, albeit in simplified form.

Pintade car mascot, in clear and
frosted glass, modeled in the form
of a guinea hen and mounted on a
square section black onyx base.
Molded mark "R. Lalique France,"
also wheel-cut "R. Lalique France."
12cm high. This fully-figural mascot,
like the frog, is very rare today.

110

Tête de paon mascot in clear, frosted and pink-stained glass in the form of a peacock's head. Intaglio-molded "R. Lalique." 17.5cm high. One of the most commanding and dramatic of Lalique's car mascot designs, with its proud crest, carefully worked feathers and curving beak, this is also a subject that recurs throughout Lalique's career, from his earliest jewelry designs. This model was created in 1928 and was also available in a vivid blue.

Longchamp car mascot in clear and frosted glass in the shape of a horse's head. Molded mark "R. Lalique France." 12cm high. Created in 1929, this is conceived in a more stylized Art Deco style than the fish or frog mascots, with its geometrically regular mane and its linear features.

These two figures are the *Moyenne Nue* statuette (right), in clear, frosted and sepia-stained glass, modeled as a draped female figure. Engraved "R. Lalique." 14 cm high. This figure and its pair, the *Moyenne Voilée* (left), were both first created in 1912 and were made both in opalescent and in colored glass. Sometimes seen as Lalique's response to the 19th-century Spanish artist Goya's paintings of *The Maja Naked* and *The Maja Clothed*, these statuettes rather reflect the continuing influence of classical Greek art in Lalique's work. The *Moyenne Voilée* statuette, in clear and frosted glass, modeled as a draped female figure holding a cup. Incised "R. Lalique France." 13.5cm. Pair to the *Moyenne Nue* statuette and modeled in the same year, 1912, the flowing drapery of this neoclassical figure is more solidly modeled, partly concealing the figure's carefully and sensuously observed curves.

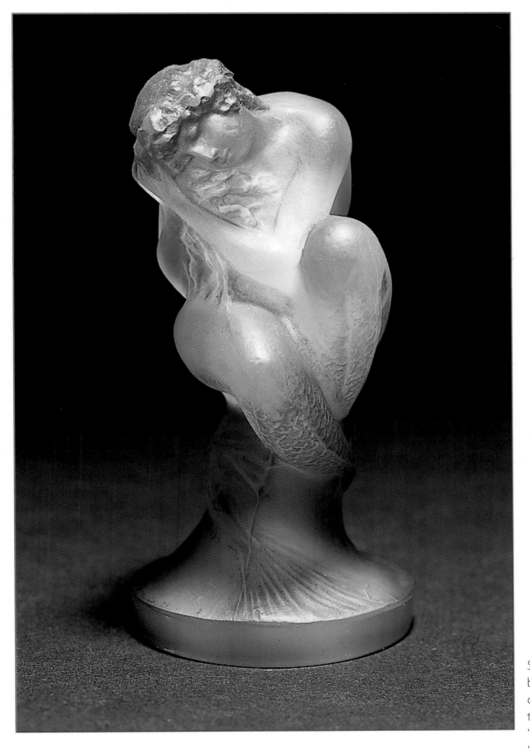

Sirène statuette in opalescent and blue-stained glass, modeled as a crouching mermaid holding flowers to the side of her face. Engraved "R. Lalique France," molded mark "R. Lalique." 10cm high. The mythological theme of the fish-tailed woman is one that appears regularly in Lalique's work. This model also served as a car mascot, and the same motif reappears in both vases and tableware. Created in 1920, this figure also draws on the classical Greek motif of the goddess Aphrodite crouching as she dries herself after the bath.

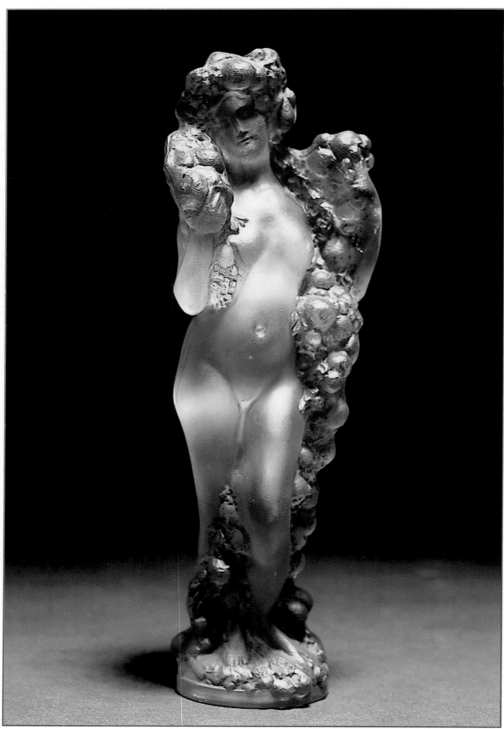

114

Figurine avec Guirlande de Fruits statuette, in frosted and gray-stained glass, modeled as a rather stubby naked female figure with a large garland of fruit and flowers falling across her shoulders to her feet, almost like drapery. Wheel-cut "R. Lalique." 21cm high. Created in 1912, the carefully three-dimensional molding of the flowers and fruit on this model is reminiscent of Lalique's earlier *cire perdue* work, and may well be a press-molded version of a unique *cire perdue* piece that is now lost.

Faucon car mascot in dark amethyst (almost black) glass, in the form of a falcon. Molded "R. Lalique," etched number. 15.5cm high. Created in 1925, this is yet another of Lalique's bird subjects, fully modeled in the round, but with a stylized head similar to that of the sparrowhawk mascot.

Pages 116–17: Topaz glass *Artichaut* (artichoke) brule-parfum base and four *Anemone* decorative motifs (three *ouverte* and one *fermée*). 11cm in diameter, the clear, frosted and black-enameled decorative motifs are modeled as flowers.

Far Right: *Le Jour et la Nuit* clock in topaz-colored glass, a rare and very valuable item first created in 1926. Disc-shaped and mounted on a silvered bronze chamfered rectangular foot, it is modeled in relief and intaglio, with a male and female nude who twine round the clock face. The female, shown with long, flowing, formalized hair, is darker in color than the male and represents night; she seems to flee from the male's outstretched arms as the night gives way to the rising sun. Acid-stenciled signature "R. Lalique." 37.5cm high.

Right: A *Chantilly* candlestick in clear, frosted and sepia-stained glass, a late creation, dating from 1943. It has a tapering stem and a square rim, intaglio-molded with a zigzagging and interlaced leaf design which is reminiscent of classical decorative motifs. Engraved "Lalique France."

Under this classification are included boxes and desk accessories, decorative household items such as mirrors, ashtrays, clocks and picture frames, as well as some mention of the more largescale architectural commissions that Lalique undertook in the 1920s and 1930s.

Small decorative boxes, used either for sweets or as a toilet accessory — e.g. for face powder — constituted the first category of works of art that Lalique produced in commercial series, from about 1910. The first examples, such as the *Deux Anges* box shown on page 128, were displayed in the Place Vendôme showroom or at the *Salon des Artistes Décorateurs*. Such small containers made of decorative or precious materials had a long tradition, from classical Rome to the ivory caskets of medieval Europe and the celadon boxes of Sung Dynasty China. Lalique's earliest boxes, made in his goldsmithing years, are one-of-a-kind pieces, made in gold, silver, copper and other precious metals, with glass and enameling decoration. Post-war pieces produced in series are most commonly circular in shape, apart from the group of rectangular cigarette boxes, and display familiar themes, such as the beetles on the *Quatre Scarabées* box and the butterflies on the *Quatre Papillons* box (see page 126).

These same themes reappear on the group of related desk accessories that Lalique designed, such as inkwells, seals, bookends, paperweights and ashtrays. Thus there is a *Trois Papillons* inkwell that is a variation on the design of the box with the same name; a *Tête de l'Aigle* seal that uses the same design as the car mascot of the same name; a *Trois Sirènes* inkwell that uses the same twining sea-nymphs as are featured on the *Ondine* and *Calypso* table services or the *Deux Sirènes* box. The sub-

stantial group of ashtrays that Lalique created also made ingenious use of the same decorative motifs. The great majority of these were made in two pieces, the generic round ashtray and a decorative element that had already served as a model for a car mascot or a perfume stopper. Examples here are *Renard* (Fox), and *Moineau* (Sparrow) shown on page 122. Simpler ashtrays without the additional figure tend to display either floral/animal motifs, such as *Anna*, with its songbird decoration and *Martinique* with its flowerheads, or a more characteristically Art Deco geometric patterning.

In addition to this small-scale work, which can quite regularly be found in salerooms, Lalique also undertook some substantial furniture and architectural commissions which are much rarer. These include a series of glass panels commissioned by the *Compagnie Internationale des Wagons-Lits* for their luxury railcars; the huge illuminated fountains discussed in the Lighting section; a number of glass doors and panels for doors, tables, screens and complete designs for the liner *Normandie* and for St. Matthew's church in Jersey

One of a pair of *Soudan* candle-sticks in clear and frosted glass, first made in 1934 in solid geometrical style. Their square bodies are molded with a zigzag banding which dictates the zigzag shape of the rim. Stencil mark "R. Lalique France."

Marguerite, a single long-stemmed
bowl-style candlestick in clear,
frosted and green-stained glass. The
wide bowl is molded as a single
daisy head, the petals lapping up
the side. Incised "R. Lalique France,"
molded "R. Lalique."

A selection of Lalique's figural ash-tray designs, which were made in two parts and then heat-molded together. Clockwise from top left:

Naïade features the mermaid figure also used as a car mascot and on tableware and vase designs. First made in 1930, this design has a round bowl and a central rectangular panel molded with the figure of a single mermaid whose legs, unusually, taper off into two fishtails and whose hair swirls out into streams of bubbles.

Moineau, also molded in two pieces, bears the hunched figure of a sparrow molded in the round, in amber glass above a circular bowl. Etched "R. Lalique."

Statuette de la Fontaine, an adaptation of a model made for the 1925 Exposition.

Caravelle, made in clear and frosted glass, has a central semicircular panel molded with a three-masted ship under full sail.

Renard, in clear and opalescent glass, carries the figure of a crouching fox, modeled in the round but in a geometrical and stylized form. It was also used as a car mascot design. Incised "R. Lalique France."

122

Merles et Raisins frosted glass
panel, a rare example of one of
the designs that Lalique created for
the *Compagnie International des
Wagons-Lits*. First made in 1928, it
was mounted in a wooden frame.
The decoration shows angular and
predatory blackbirds on a grape-
laden vine.

This selection of decorative boxes shows the wide range of shapes and designs that Lalique could draw on. Clockwise from left:

Chat, clear and frosted rectangular box with cover, bearing a cat's face molded in low relief. The design is unusual among Lalique's boxes which more commonly bear floral or geometric designs. Etched mark "Lalique France."

Dahlia, a circular box and cover in frosted and black-enameled glass, which was made as part of a toilet garniture also comprising two scent bottles. The box is modeled as a   single flowerhead.

Fakhry Pacha square cigarette box, made in clear, frosted and sepia-stained glass. It was commissioned by Fakhry Pacha, uncle to the King Fouad I of Egypt, and bears the king's portrait. The sides are molded with Egyptian motifs, and the base is inscribed "*Offert par Fakhry Pacha à Paris, le 9 Octobre 1924*." Molded mark "R. Lalique."

Houppes, a round box in clear, frosted and opalescent glass, its lid molded with dandelions. Engraved "R. Lalique France"; molded "R. Lalique."

Three round boxes which reflect Lalique's enjoyment of floral and insect motifs. Clockwise from left.

Two *Quatre Papillons* boxes, in frosted, opalescent and blue-stained glass, with their lids molded in low relief with four symmetrically placed butterflies, and the base with stylized flowering trees. Created in 1911, this is an early design which reappears on other items, such as the inkwell illustrated later in this section. Engraved "R. Lalique No. 14."

Meudon, also called *Dahlias*, was first made in 1924 and is shown here in clear, frosted and gray-stained glass. The lid is molded in low relief with stylized and geometrically conceived dahlias and foliage. Molded mark "R. Lalique"; Stencil mark "Lalique France."

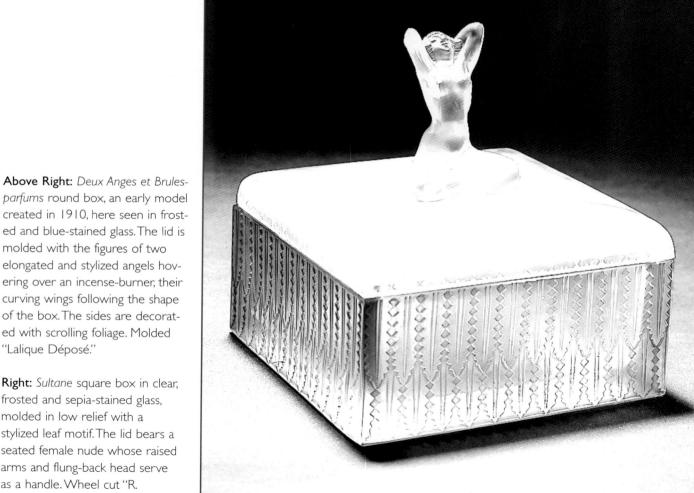

128

Above Right: *Deux Anges et Brules-parfums* round box, an early model created in 1910, here seen in frosted and blue-stained glass. The lid is molded with the figures of two elongated and stylized angels hovering over an incense-burner, their curving wings following the shape of the box. The sides are decorated with scrolling foliage. Molded "Lalique Déposé."

Right: *Sultane* square box in clear, frosted and sepia-stained glass, molded in low relief with a stylized leaf motif. The lid bears a seated female nude whose raised arms and flung-back head serve as a handle. Wheel cut "R. Lalique France."

Bluets, a clear and frosted rectangular picture frame, etched in low relief with a stylized pattern of overlapping cornflower blooms. Wheel-cut "R. Lalique France."

130

Inséparables, a clear, frosted and opalescent clock with a circular gilt and blue enamel clockface beside which perch two pairs of lovebirds on a flowering cherry branch. Only 11 cm high, this is the smallest of Lalique's clock designs and was first made in 1926. Molded mark "R. Lalique"; engraved "France."

Most of Lalique's designs for ashtrays were conceived between 1920 and 1932; these all date from the 1920s and show the range of Lalique's repertoire. From left to right and top to bottom:

Jamaique, a round ashtray in clear and frosted glass, its rim decorated with a textural leaf and berry motif which curls up over the edges and gives a slight angularity to the round shape. The motif is reminiscent of the egg and dart decoration which was a regular feature of classical Greek temple design. Engraved "Lalique France."

Fauvettes, a star-shaped design in clear and frosted glass. An octagonal bowl is set within the star shape, creating a rim formed of triangular elements. These are molded in low relief with naturalistic birds and foliage. Intaglio-molded "R. Lalique France No.289."

Martinique, in clear, frosted and blue-stained glass. Its rim is molded in low relief with eight stylized flower-heads seen in profile and set between clear panels. The flowerheads are three-dimensional, and their petals continue the decoration down the sides of the ahstray. Engraved "R. Lalique France."

Anna, a clear and frosted ashtray, square with beviled corners, with both the base and the rim decorated with a motif of small birds perched on branches, similar in conception to the design of *Fauvettes*.

Tabago, a round ashtray in clear and frosted glass, its rim molded in low relief with a leaf design on which sit a ring of scarab beetles. This slightly macabre motif recalls Lalique's use of similarly grotesque decorative themes in his early days as a jeweller. Engraved "R. Lalique France."

Alice, an octagonal ashtray in clear and frosted glass, the rim molded in low relief with stylized and curvaceous dancing figures set in oval frames surrounded by graduated curving lines. The formalized nature of this design forms a contrast to the more naturalistic bird motifs seen on other ashtrays here. Engraved mark "R. Lalique France No. 289."

Vézelay, four examples of this square design, all in clear and frosted glass. The bowl is also square, set at right angles within the rim, and the whole is decorated with geometrically-positioned lacy vine leaves. Molded mark "R. Lalique."

Grenade, a round ashtray in clear and frosted glass, the rim decorated with pyramidal shapes which emerge from bands of formalized foliage. Engraved "R. Lalique France."

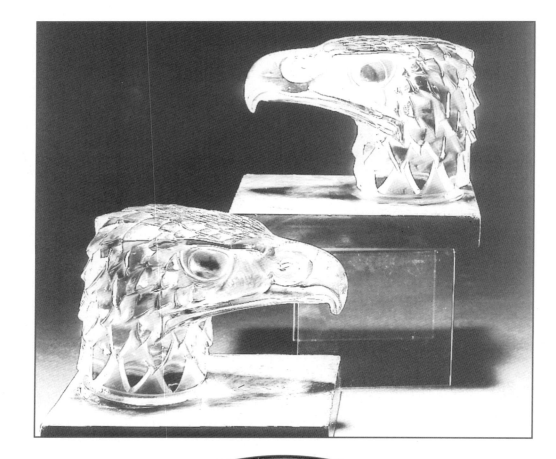

132

Above Right: *Tête de l'Aigle* book-ends, in clear and frosted glass. Conceived as an eagle's head set on a rectangular base, this imposing design can also be found as a car mascot and a seal. Molded mark "R. Lalique France."

Right: *Trois Dahlias* box cover in clear and opalescent glass, molded in low relief with a design of three overlapping flowerheads. These decorative boxes were generally used as toilet items. Molded mark "R. Lalique."

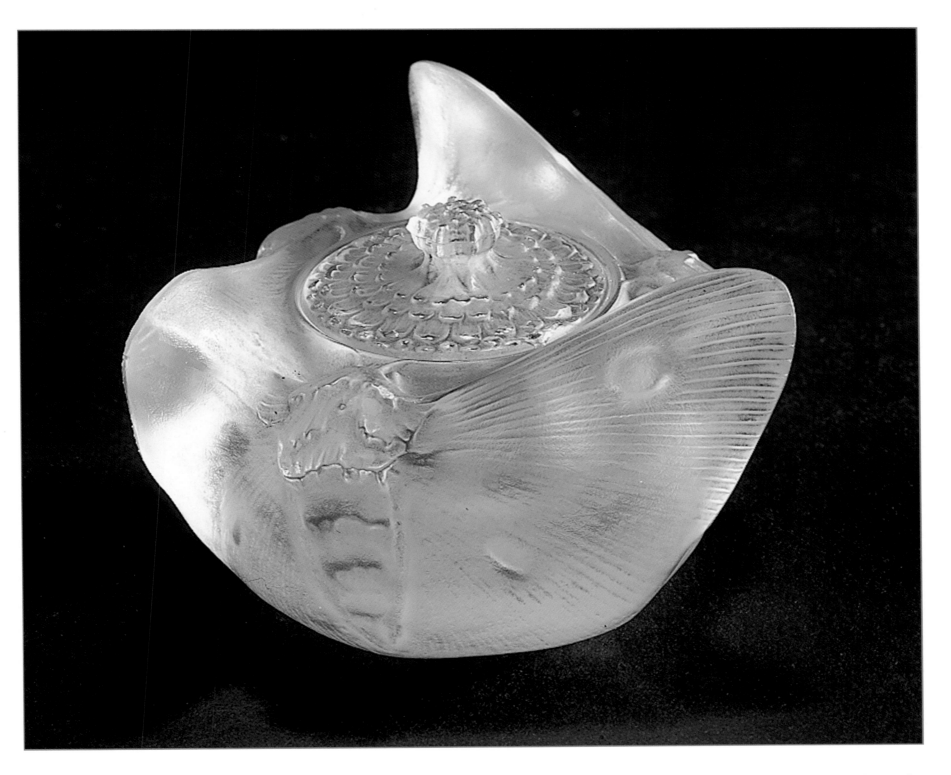

133

Trois Papillons inkwell with cover, in clear, frosted and sepia-stained glass. The asymmetrical shape of this unusual piece is created by the overlapping wings of three butterflies, gathering round the large flowerhead which forms the lid. Another early design, this was first made in 1912. Molded mark "R. Lalique."

A decorative door made in 1928 for the carriages of the Compagnie Internationale des Wagons-Lits, with three glass panels set in wood and showing three sultry nude female figures set against a background of grape-bearing vines.

Cigales box (left), in amber glass and first made in 1921, featuring the grasshopper motif which is a regularly recurring feature of Lalique's work from his earliest creations.

Camaret vase (right), another of Lalique's characteristic fish designs, this one conceived in a relatively geometric form, with rows of carefully organized plump little fish in low relief swimming in opposite directions around the curve of the vase.

The characteristic opalescent glass which was Lalique's preferred medium was particularly suited to lighting fixtures because of the innate luminosity of the glass when backlit. Although most of the table lamps and hanging lights shown here belong to Lalique's main period of lighting design in the 1920s and 1930s, the first experiments in lamp design were made as early as 1905 and in Art Nouveau style. Few of these objects themselves survive, but photographs in *L'Art Decoratif*, a design magazine of the period, include a bronze and glass chandelier decorated with lizards, and a hanging light composed of 12 bronze chameleons, six positioned vertically to hold the light's glass panels and the other six poised to spring on the unwary passer-by below.

It was only after the move to Wingen in 1918, however, that lighting devices became a regular feature of Lalique's repertoire. Domestic electricity was becoming more widely available in the post-war period, and as ever Lalique recognized and responded to this new market, creating table lamps, wall brackets, hanging lights and massive decorative chandeliers for the tall ceilings of the period. Most of these were made using the press-molding technique, and tonal gradations obtained by varying the thickness of the glass. Many of them adopted decorative themes found in other areas of Lalique's *oeuvre*, such as the *Feuilles de Murier* (mulberry leaves) table lamp of 1927 or the *Soleil* (sun) hanging light of 1926, while some were designed in a more thorough-going geometric Art Deco style. Today Lalique vases can be found which have been transformed into lamps, such as the *Ronces* (briars) lamp shown top left, but Lalique never intended them for this purpose. He did, however, adapt some of his statuettes into lights — the famous *Suzanne* can be found in illuminated form, as can some of the small car mascots, and the lamps illustrated on the following pages were designed originally as statuettes.

The hanging globes and chandeliers are among some of Lalique's most significant design achievements. Not only are these works of art in their own right, but they are also ingeniously created to diffuse the light through their molded surface and to use the ceiling as a reflector in order to create a two-toned effect. A more elaborate piece might also be cut and polished, or particular areas of the design treated with acid to produce a clear, frosted or milky effect.

Among these is the impressive series of lamps known as *tiara veuilleuse*, designed to look like perfume bottles with overflowing stoppers, such as the *Perruches* lamp on page 141. Other exotic items included illuminated tables, of which the surviving few are collector's items, and a series of illuminated fountains, notably the huge *Les Sources de France* that Lalique created for the 1925 Exposition of Modern Decorative and Industrial Arts and which consisted of 17 tiers of frosted glass panels, each bearing eight *Source de la Fontaine* statuettes.

Pages 136–37: *Feuilles de Murier* table lamp in frosted glass (detail). See page 142.

Far Left, Above: This is the *Ronces* vase discussed in the Vases section, converted into an electrical fitting. The ovoid vase shape was particularly suited to this form of adaptation and examples are common, both from the period when Lalique was working and more recently. The design is of interlacing briars, relief molded "R. Lalique."

Far Left, Below: *Nanking* spherical *plafonnier* or ceiling light molded all over with a geometric design of graduated triangles.

Left: *Six Danseuses* table lamp, in clear, frosted and blue-stained glass. The tapering circular shade is molded in low relief with a frieze of classically-gowned nymphs against a background of twining garlands, and the footed cylindrical stem is molded with the same garland design. Stencil mark "R. Lalique France." 25.5cm high. Created in 1931 specifically as a lamp design, this piece is conceived in a relatively naturalistic figurative manner; most of Lalique's lighting designs take a more stylized form.

The two table lamps shown here are examples of a rare, and today not particularly popular, category in Lalique's work, that of religious subjects. In the 1930s he created a number of pieces, principally panels and pendants, with subjects drawn from Christian imagery. The commonest themes, as can be seen here, were the Crucifixion and the Virgin and Child, and many of the larger pieces in this category were subsequently converted into lamps. On the left is the *Vierge et l'Enfant* table light, in clear and frosted glass, formed from a rectangular panel intaglio-molded with a figure of the Virgin holding the Child, and set within a chrome base. Stencil mark "R. Lalique France." 40cm high. The original design was first created in 1937, relatively late in Lalique's career and around the time he was working on his most major religious commission, the church of St. Matthew on the island of Jersey (see Introduction). The rigidly frontal pose of the Virgin and the stylized folds of the garments worn by both figures reflects the influence of archaic Greek sculpture on Art Deco designs.

On the right is a *Christ* table lamp, in clear and frosted glass, modeled with the figure of Christ on the cross and mounted on a patinated metal tapering rectangular base. Stencil mark "R. Lalique France." 23cm high.

Perruches table lamp, 41cm high, a form of lighting described in the company catalog as a *veilleuse*. Among Lalique's most valued and collectable creations, these items are conceived as conical or quadrangular bases with an electric fitting inside, so that the base is the light source. The decorative element is designed as a form of elaborate bottle stopper, reminiscent of some of Lalique's perfume bottles. In this case the stopper element is intaglio-molded with three pairs of love-birds or parakeets, perched on interlaced blossoming branches, a theme which reappears as a vase, a clock and a bowl. Stencil mark "R. Lalique France."

Voilées Mains Jointes table lamp. Again this is a converted piece; the original statuette was created in 1919 and conceived as a classically draped and veiled female figure, reminiscent of archaic Greek sculpture in her hieratic frontality and rigidity, with her hands clasped to one side of her face. It has been subsequently wired and fitted into a chrome metal base. 34cm high.

142

Faisans candelabra, a pair of clear and frosted multiple candlesticks, in the form of a footed bowl bearing four circular candle-holders. The interior of the bowl is molded with a low-relief design of pheasants and floral garlands. Engraved "Lalique France."

Feuilles de Murier table lamp in frosted glass. The circular base carries a ribbed cylindrical column, which in turn supports a clear glass bowl molded in relief with a design of skeletal mulberry leaves which appear to emerge from the glass. This example is unmarked, but the identical design is numbered 2163 in the *catalogue raisonné*. 36cm high. Made in three parts and then assembled, this is a characteristically inventive example of Lalique's lighting work.

Detail of a *Sirène plafonnier* or hanging light in opalescent glass, molded in low relief with a design of a sinuous mermaid whose curving fishtail echoes the curving lines of bubbles which surround her. Originally designed as a piece of tableware, this has been drilled and fitted with suspension hooks to convert it into a ceiling light shade. Molded "R. Lalique."

Above from left: *Dahlias plafonnier* or hanging light, in frosted glass. Molded in low relief with a design of flowers and foliage, this was probably originally designed as a bowl, as the gilt bronze hanging frame is of later date. Wheel-cut "R. Lalique."

Coquilles plafonnier or hanging light, in opalescent glass molded in low relief in a design of overlapping stylized clam shells. Wheel-cut "R. Lalique." The shell motif featured regularly in Lalique's repertoire, on vases, tableware and boxes, generally in this geometrically conceived Art Deco form.

Soleil plafonnier, in opaque and blue-stained glass, and with a design of interwoven sunflowers.

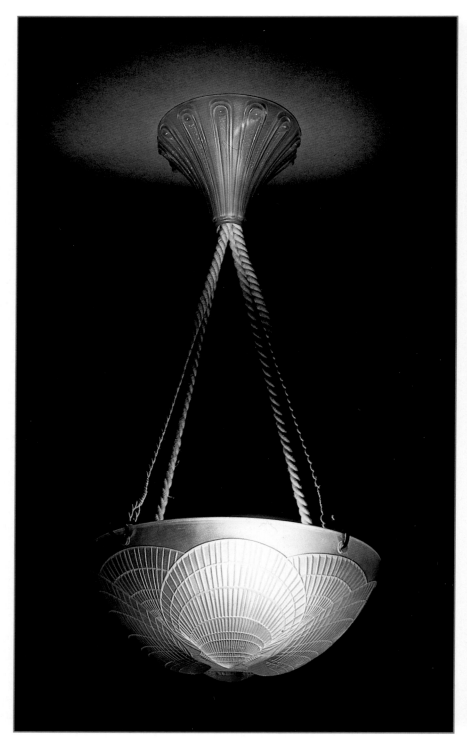

144

Dahlias plafonnier, in opalescent glass, molded in low relief with a pattern of protuberant flower-heads.

Rinceaux plafonnier, an elegantly geometric Art Deco design, first made in 1926 and here seen in amber-colored glass.